The Shoebox Effect

"Marcie Keithley is no stranger to love and loss. She has boarded that train more than once. In this part-memoir, part-survival guide, she invites and empowers the reader to navigate the murky waters of trauma and to transform experiences that can otherwise impede our joy and block our evolution. Go ahead . . . grab that shoebox and let Marcie inspire you to become your best self."

—Rhonda Churchill, LPC
Author of *The Fifth and Final Name:*
Memoir of an American Churchill

"Safekeeping in any type of 'shoebox' is okay as long as it isn't harming you or anyone else, but what if it is? Marcie Keithley writes with compassion and passion as she explores what it is like to hold in life-long secrets and why truths must be told in order to feel free and complete. Her goal is to guide the willing reader away from shame and feeling manipulated and toward transparency, dignity, and self-acceptance."

—Paige L. Adams Strickland, Teacher,
Author of *Akin to the Truth: A Memoir of Adoption and Identity*
and *After The Truth*

"An important story to tell, Marcie Keithley has written a must-read primer for anyone on a journey of healing and self-discovery. We all have shoeboxes tucked away, but this compelling read not only offers insight and hope, it also gives us direction in opening our own shoeboxes to promote authenticity in our own journeys."

—Pamela Karanova, Founder, Adoptees Connect Inc.

"It's true we all have our secrets. We tuck pieces of ourselves and our lives away, the parts of us we don't want to see. But for those of us in the adoption triad, we have vital pieces that are not only hidden—they are missing. In *The Shoebox Effect*, author Marcie J. Keithley gives readers the hope and courage it takes to open our own boxes through her story. This book will shake loose the lies behind the industry and set hearts free. A must-read for anyone touched by adoption."

—Rhonda Robinson, Adoptee, Speaker, Author of
FreeFall: Holding Onto Faith When the Unthinkable Strikes

"In *The Shoebox Effect*, Marcie J. Keithley reminds us that what we hide may be the secret to self-realization and ultimately joy."

—Anne Heffron
Award Winning Screenwriter, Writing Coach
and Author of *You Don't Look Adopted*

"*The Shoebox Effect* is an amazing story of love, sorrow, loss, redemption and triumph. Through Marcie's beautiful and heartfelt writing, she takes you on a journey that tugs at your heartstrings. This engaging story keeps you turning the page, wondering what will happen next. What makes it even more incredible is that this powerful story isn't the product of some great fiction writer. It's a true, unembellished story that continues to unfold. This is a must read."

—Vanessa Collins
Minister, Author, Writing and Publishing Coach

"*The Shoebox Effect* explores the question of whether or not behavior, like an heirloom, can be passed from one generation to another. Marcie J. Keithley uncovers a multigenerational family pathology of mothers leaving daughters. The secrets found inside the family shoebox is where the typical adoption story begins . . . and ends."

—Patti Hawn
Entertainment Publicist, Author of *Good Girls Don't*
Sister of Legendary Film Actress, Goldie Hawn

"We all love a story about ordinary, everyday people that when faced with challenges or extraordinary circumstances, hang on and find the way to fight . . . and win the day. They become heroes. Marcie is one; the kind our world needs to hear about."

—Dennis Lowery
President Adducent Inc, Author, Writer, International Speaker

"An avid reader, I have read many books in my lifetime. As a friend of Marcie's, I have known a good portion of her story as well. Knowing what I do though, did not prepare me for the emotional reaction I felt while reading. Fair warning: You must read with tissues close by because *The ShoeBox Effect* will cause your eyes to get misty! I'm so very excited for Marcie's story to receive a broader audience, and for people to find help and healing from their wounds, as she shares her compelling story."

—Victoria Duerstock
Author, Speaker, Musician
Heart & Home Design Basics for Your Soul & Living Space

"*The Shoebox Effect* reads like a fascinating memoir, but is also filled with life-changing thoughts, tips and transformations you expect from a great nonfiction read. Knowing this is an unimaginable true story makes it even more of a page-turner.

I especially liked the way the author helped me unpack my own shoe-boxes at the end of each chapter and offered many great side-bar notes."

—Anita Agers Brooks
International Speaker, Inspirational Business/Life Coach
Award-Winning Author of *Getting Through What You Can't Get Over*

"In *The ShoeBox Effect,* Marcie Keithley takes us on a journey of her life's painful losses, beginning with her mother at age five. As a confused and again abandoned young woman, she succumbed to the tragic loss of her own child to adoption. Keithley reveals her emergence from denial and suppression as she opens her shoeboxes of mementoes and confronts her pain with courage and fortitude. As she faces her own personal demons, she adds to her story by offering us, her readers, questions and guidance for how we may do the same, leading to our own transformation and healing."

—Linda Franklin
Licensed Clinical Social Worker, Psychotherapist
Author of *I'll Always Carry You*

"A riveting and exquisitely told story. *The Shoebox Effect* is sublime in that it not only inspires through its author's rich reveal of family secrets, but through its unique invitation and roadmap for the reader to do the same. Anyone delving into their past to heal their present could ask for no better guide than Marcie Keithley."

—Suzanne Bachner & Bob Brader, Award-Winning Writers
The Good Adoptee & *Spitting in The Face of The Devil*

THE

SHOEBOX

EFFECT

The Shoebox Effect: Transforming Pain Into Fortitude and Purpose
Marcie J. Keithley

Brookstone Publishing Group
P.O. Box 211, Evington, VA 24550
BrookstoneCreativeGroup.com

Ordering Information:
Special discounts are available on quantity purchases by corporations,
associations, and others. For details, contact
Brookstone Publishing Group at the address above.

ISBN: 978-1-949856-17-0 (print), 978-1-949856-18-7 (epub)

Author's Note: In writing *The Shoebox Effect*, I consulted with most of the people who appear in the book, and called upon my own memory of these events and the time it covers in my life. I have changed the names and modified identifying details of some, but not all, of the individuals in this book in order to protect their anonymity. There are not any composite characters or events in this book. I occasionally omitted people and events, but only when that omission had no impact on either the veracity or the substance of the story.

THE
SHOEBOX EFFECT

TRANSFORMING PAIN INTO FORTITUDE AND PURPOSE

MARCIE J. KEITHLEY

Foreword by Dr. Joyce Maguire Pavao, EdD, LCSW

For my sister Judy
and all of those still living their lives in a box.

*May you find the strength to face the things within your box,
and all that limits your life.*

*Freedom comes from taking control of the past—
don't let it hold power over you.*

CONTENTS

FOREWORD

Dr. Joyce Maguire Pavao
Lecturer in Psychiatry, Harvard Medical School
Author of *The Family of Adoption,* Beacon Press

There is a natural, magnetic field around like-minded adoption reform advocates. I've lived in adoption for seventy-three years, and I've worked in the adoption field for forty-five years. I founded two clinics that have nothing to do with adoption placement, but rather everything to do with the education, consulting, training, and treatment for those who live in adoption. As an adoption reform advocate, I often find that people confuse this role as being anti-adoption. This simply is not true. I advocate for ethical, legal, safe, and sincere adoptions for all who choose adoption. Marcie J. Keithley is one of these fellow advocates. She has worked very hard to educate and bring people together in this complex world of adoption. *The Shoebox Effect* is one of the many ways she has brought light to this subject.

The Shoebox Effect is a multi-generational story of secrecy and silence. It is a story about the evolving of women in the home and in the workplace. It is a story about human and emotional development. It is a story of loss, trauma, and facing your demons. It is a story of hopelessness as well as hope. It is a story of family, in all of its broken and fragmented pieces. It is a story of opening Pandora's box.

The Shoebox Effect expertly weaves trauma and pain from the past into the present, giving hope for the future. Through Keithley's story, readers will learn what works and what doesn't work in light of *The Shoebox Effect*. Marcie opens up her heart along with all of her tucked-away shoeboxes in order to decompartmentalize and integrate her story and her life. By inviting others into her world, readers experience the freedom to consider their own confined and constrained segments of life that could use some airing out and exploration. *The Shoebox Effect* is like the "Marie Kondo" of emotions and secrets.

Fair warning, reader—you may not want to read *The Shoebox Effect* in a public place. From chapter one and throughout the story, you'll want to have tissues handy.

I believe *The Shoebox Effect* is cathartic, not only for the writer, but the reader as well. We all have our own shoeboxes.

Marcie's story reminds me of a poem I wrote years ago titled "Pandora: I Collect Boxes." The following is an excerpt of that poem that I believe parallels with Marcie's story, *The Shoebox Effect*.

Pandora: I Collect Boxes

Pandora may have found unsettling things,
But inside the box was the truth.
Frightening and chaotic—but the truth.
And when she reopened the box a second time,
There was Hope along with the Truth.
It was all there, waiting,
   whether she opened that box or not.
It held more power unrevealed
   than it did once revealed.
Open all the lids!
Let the secrets fly!
Let the joys and sorrows fly!
Open all the lids!
Open all the hearts!
Open all the minds!
Open all that is your own,
Because at the bottom
Of the box,
Once opened,
And twice reopened again,
Is Hope.

—Joyce Maguire Pavao, 1996

PROLOGUE

Most of us have one, or something similar hidden away. That box filled with reminders of a past we long to revisit. That box we shove into a corner, hoping it will help conceal the memories from our minds. And for some of us, that shoebox keeps our secrets.

As I tell you my story of opening not just one, but three hidden boxes, and the powerful effects their contents have had on multiple lives, I want you to consider the heart of my motives. See, writing this book isn't about me—it's about you—the reader. After I've spoken on the shoebox effect, people of various ages, regions, backgrounds, and positions want to tell me about their boxes, whether their collections are kept in an actual shoebox or not.

What we put in our shoeboxes, or what we discover in someone else's, can alter the course of our entire lives, as has been the case for me. It started with one of the greatest losses I've ever known.

I sat on my garage floor and wondered for the umpteenth time, *How could my sister be gone?*

Judy kept assuring us she was fine—she said her cough was nothing to be concerned about—until she could hide it no longer. By the time we knew there was an urgency, it was too late. We wouldn't even make it to say our final goodbyes in person. However, God gave us a gift before she died.

My sister had already slipped into unconsciousness. She hadn't awoken since Thursday. My niece called to give us an update on

Saturday—Judy's birthday. My mom, brother, step-father, and I were on speaker phone when we heard it.

"Sh. Listen," my brother said.

The three of us huddled closer toward the phone. At first, all we could hear was a muffled gurgle. Seconds later, the sound transformed into a strained rasp. Mommy (I still call her that today) grabbed the phone and shouted, "Judy, honey, it's Mama. I'm here. I love you!"

We could hear Judy take a heavy breath. Then in a very slow and measured response, graveled as her voice was, my sister said, "I. Love. You. Mama."

Mommy's emotions were written in the pink tinge on her cheeks and the tears flowing to her chin. She handed the phone to me.

I clutched the receiver and said, "It's me. It's your sissy. I love you, Jute."

The deep breaths coming through the receiver let us know how much effort my sister was exerting. But she was determined. The last words my sister spoke came in that precious moment when she drew out the words, "I. Love. You. Sissy." Then we heard a rustling sound.

My niece came back on. "I'm sorry. She's getting restless. I've got to go." The line went dead.

Our little family sat still and silent. Numb. So happy Judy had been able to speak—so sad because we felt what was coming. In five days, I no longer had my sister.

Two years later, the blanket of grief and guilt that draped over me still felt smothering. But as I sat in my garage, I knew what I had to do.

I finally garnered my courage to look through the only possessions I had left from Judy's past. I took a deep breath and said, "Oh, Sissy. Oh, my sweet sissy." Then I pulled the lid off of the burgundy tote.

Inside were photos of Judy's grandchildren, drawings and paintings her daughter and grandson had given her, pictures of some of the properties she'd managed, and old business cards. But separated from the other mementos was a small, plain box. When I opened it and looked inside, I discovered a secret letter written in pencil. I read it.

"What?" I said to the empty garage. My shaking hands rattled the edges of the yellowed, forty-nine-year-old piece of paper.

In shock, I read it again. "I can't believe this," I said out loud. I scanned the note one more time to ensure I was really seeing the words I thought I'd read. Then I put everything back inside the little box. I cradled it under my arm as I got into my car. Mommy and I needed to have a serious talk.

I understand what I know about the shoebox effect today, but it didn't make the impact any less powerful. Some surprises turn everything upside down.

CHAPTER ONE

THE DAY DREYFUS DIED

Have you ever wondered why human beings are prone to cram snippets of life experiences inside little square containers? And then, to make the habit more confusing, why we tend to ignore or avoid these mementos for long periods of time?

It's as if by sequestering tokens, trinkets, or symbols, we can keep our thoughts and emotions under control, tightly lidded inside a box—at least that's what I tried to do. But eventually, someone or something has a way of making us release what we've held back for so long. In my case, Dreyfus kicked the lid right off of my box. Literally and metaphorically.

I prolonged the decision to put my dog down just as I had avoided signing the divorce papers lying on my kitchen desk. By ignoring the documents, I somehow reasoned that I hadn't failed and wasn't really throwing my seventeen-year marriage away. In the same way, by not allowing myself to think about what the vet had said, I tried to convince myself that my beloved pet did not have a golf-ball-sized tumor on his left front leg.

Denial. My go-to. I covered it with a veneer—a facade—but it was still denial. Over the years, I had become the master of concealment. And the very thing that would rip the cover off my masquerade appeared to me that evening—disguised in fur.

When I pulled my Lexus into the driveway after work, I watched for the familiar face of my golden boy to appear in my home office window. Even though we'd only lived in the new house for three months, Dreyfus had a set routine. The move was necessary for two reasons.

I had asked my husband of seventeen years for a divorce, and Dreyfus, my dog, could no longer walk up or down the steps in our previous home. As much as I had loved our place on Shetland Court in Southern Indiana and all it represented, I longed to move on with my life as a newly single woman at fifty-two-years old. A new house represented my new life.

On this day, I got out of my car and walked toward the front door, still looking for the loving face of my pet—someone I could always count on. I thought it odd he was not in his usual place waiting for me. He knew when to expect me home from my job as a bank manager. His wet nose was always pressed against the window until he heard me unlock the front door. But not tonight. Still no sign of him.

Inside, I called out, "Dreyfus. Come here, boy," thinking he didn't hear me pull up.

When I got no response, I headed to my office, but found it empty. I called again. "Dreyfus? Where are you, buddy?"

A sick feeling of panic turned my stomach sour as I searched the house. But my precious Dreyfus was still missing. I walked to the laundry room, thinking perhaps I had left the door to the garage open that morning. It was then I heard a sound coming from the master bedroom. This was the last place I expected to find him.

Dreyfus had full use of the house with one exception, my bedroom was the only off-limits room. This rule had been in place since the day we picked him up from the breeder in Terre Haute. My second husband had stated firmly, "No dogs in our bedroom."

So Dreyfus would lay outside our room with his nose as close to the doorway as possible, but he never entered. The rule in the new house was no different. When I realized he was in my room, alarms immediately went off in my head.

I hurried down the hall, quickly making the short walk through my bedroom, and found Dreyfus in my walk-in closet. He was curled in a corner surrounded by my many boxes of shoes. He had nuzzled them out of his way to make a comfortable space for himself. The floor around Dreyfus resembled a department store after Black Friday morning.

I knew something was wrong. And it wasn't the mess that made my stomach clench.

"What's the matter, buddy?" I said softly. "What are you doing in here?"

I knelt down and joined him on the floor. Burying my face in his yellow fur, I told him over and over again, "I love you so much. You know how much I love you, don't you, boy? Hang on, you're going to be okay. You've got to be okay. I need you."

But inside, I knew the truth. This was my pet's way of telling me it was time; he couldn't take the pain anymore. Dreyfus had gone into my room and entered my closet, the one place he was not allowed, to show me he was ready to die. He knew I would not be strong enough to make the decision to put him down on my own. So, he did something uncharacteristic to make sure I knew he needed me to end his suffering.

As I sat with my back against the wall, holding Dreyfus in my arms, I looked at the total disarray around me. Then, one particular box caught my eye. I had hidden it away long ago.

I always kept the old shoebox out of sight, but now, it lay on its side, still tied shut with an aging ribbon—a birthday gift from long ago. I didn't have to lift the lid to find out what was inside. I winced as I recalled its contents. The pain of the memories inside were as fresh as the day I left the hospital on that cold, November afternoon.

Feeling sorry for myself, I contemplated what the box symbolized. Just as God was not healing my pet now, over the years, He had not silenced the memory of my baby's cries. He had also let Roger leave me with a broken heart.

Though it occurred decades before, even before my marriage that had just ended, I was haunted by the echo of my former love's footsteps as they receded. I had never fully recovered after he walked away from our child and me. Though he left us, my heart held on to a piece of him—it felt as if I had seen him only yesterday. The memory of his hot breath whispering into my ear, "I love you more," made me shudder.

I'd tried everything to move on. Hiding Roger's abandonment away as if it never happened hadn't worked. The ghost of that memory, one I'd tried to exorcise, freshly awakened as I held my Dreyfus. The past and the present now tormented me simultaneously. Sitting among the boxes of shoes and next to my box of secrets, I rocked as I held my dying dog.

I cried out to the ceiling, "Make it stop. Dear God, make it stop." I clung to my poor, innocent pet. His sweet face, so loving, so pure, reminded me of that helpless moment on a cold, blustery day when I lost my little girl.

Saying Goodbye

"Let me know when you're ready," Dr. Brown said softly as she prepared the shot. I looked into the moist eyes of my veterinarian, who had graciously agreed to come to my home for something I did not want to happen.

"Grandma?" I heard the sweet voice of my fourteen-year-old granddaughter, Mackaila. "Grandma, are you ready?"

Always protective of her six-year-old brother, Mackaila added, "Zane can't be here though, Grandma. He's way too little." Mackaila fiercely protected her youngest sibling, a sweet boy with smiling gray eyes like his mother's, and laughter that warms the heart.

Earlier in the day, my oldest granddaughter, Chelsea, was there when Mackaila and I moved Dreyfus's bed to the middle of the living room floor. We decided that when it was his time to cross the Rainbow Bridge, he would leave us from the comfort of his own home, surrounded by those who loved him. No way was I abandoning him in a cold room at my vet's office. We knew it would be hard to see him take his final breath here, but it was the least we could do for him after all the years of joy he gave to us.

Mackaila laid on one side of him, with me on the other. Chelsea clung to her boyfriend, Billy, and stood quietly by the fireplace. We said our goodbyes and told Dreyfus what a great dog he was and how much we loved him.

Dr. Brown kneeled down, looked at me, and said gravely, "When you're ready Marcie, I am."

"Dreyfus, look at me," my granddaughter said bravely. "Look at Mackaila." I watched my grandbaby struggle to remain strong. I knew I couldn't delay it any longer. I nodded to the doctor.

"I love you buddy," I said through tears that flowed heavier when the chemical entered his body. "I love you so much. I will never forget you. Go to sleep now."

Only seconds passed and I heard Dreyfus take his last breath. He died in the arms of the two people who loved him the most. It gave me no peace.

"He's gone," Dr. Brown said softly, breaking the brief moment of silence. "I am so sorry for your loss."

Upon hearing her words, my quiet tears turned to sobs and my body shook in mourning. The two of us, Mackaila and me, arms entwined around Dreyfus, clung to his lifeless body. As I wept for the passing of my Golden, another pain struck me even harder. The loss of Dreyfus had reached into my soul and stirred something I had suppressed for years in order to survive.

Brief images of my life over the last twenty years bubbled up, including the secrets I'd tried to ignore. I'd closed them up in a box I'd hidden, and lacked the courage to confront. Throughout the years, even though I couldn't bring myself to open it, I could not get rid of my shoebox.

The Shoebox Effect

Though I was familiar with the term, in my grief-stricken state, I didn't realize I was experiencing my own shoebox effect. I learned about this concept when I began my career in the financial and insurance industry.

The shoebox effect describes plan members who pay for products or services rendered, then save the receipts for submission to the insurer for reimbursement when they have a claim. These receipts are often stored in a shoebox (or a similar container). But they are never submitted because the insured either believes they don't need them, forgets they have them, or the receipts don't amount to enough to make them worth the effort.

This reduction in claims produces a substantial financial windfall for the insurance provider from an accumulation of clients who never file. In fact, one study showed that nearly eight percent of all claims were never submitted due to the insured's forgetfulness. Out of sight, out of mind, I suppose.

As you might imagine, insurance companies are great fans of this loss to consumers. But the shoebox effect applies to humans in another very real way.

You have experiences in your everyday life—good and bad. Tangible reminders can include items like ticket stubs to that first movie you saw with your high school boyfriend, or a picture from that special concert the two of you attended for the first time. Family items are often symbolized. Remember that Christmas ornament you made for your mom in first grade?

Most of us have put mementos from our childhoods in a shoebox for safekeeping and stored them on a shelf. We may see the box from time to time, and once in a while, even take it down and ease the lid off, to stare at our memories. If they are good recollections, we might relive them in our minds, or physically clutch a souvenir to our heart, before placing it back inside the box. Not so with bad experiences.

We hide those emotional triggers away—shoving the shoebox to the very back of the highest shelf we can reach. We want to hide those old thoughts away, so we never have to face them or that pain again. But just as the insured bears the cost of lost reimbursements, there is a price to pay for what we don't face in our past. The guilt and shame that emanate from the secret box creates toxicity—eating away at us.

Whether looking at it from a financial perspective in its original meaning, or through the emotional form I'll share in this book, the shoebox effect could present a danger to people. I don't want this to happen to you.

The Shoebox Sherpa

As you'll soon discover, I've had to pull my own shoeboxes off the shelf—physically and emotionally—in order to find the freedom I desperately needed. If you are seeking peace, you will have to do the same, but you do not have to go through it alone. I am here to support and guide you. Some even call me a Shoebox Sherpa, and it is my honor to assist you, as you find the liberation you desire.

The term Sherpa is commonly used to describe someone who is a mountain guide or porter working in the Everest area. But Sherpa is actually the name of an ethnic group of people who live in the mountains of Nepal, central Asia. Sherpas are local people who are highly experienced and skilled climbers—without them, most climbers would not be able to reach the summit of a mountain[1]. It is in this spirit, through the writing of this book, I offer myself to you.

I want to help you up your metaphorical mountains. Whether you have an actual shoebox or an emotional one that you reference from time to time, the shoebox effect is a reality. You may fear facing what you've hidden inside or believe the contents aren't important enough to deal with, but I promise, you'll only experience freedom when you gain the courage to open it and take out what you've put inside.

I only learned this when grief forced me to do what I had desperately tried to avoid. Moments after Dreyfus drew his last breath, I mentally went back to the moment I found him in my room among the scattered boxes. It was then I realized no shoebox or closet was big

---

1 https://www.bbc.co.uk/newsround/27130467

enough to hide away my secrets any longer. There was no escaping the story of my life.

I unnecessarily wasted years of time and energy, allowing others to control me, and hiding from the truth. Hopefully, I can save you from making a similar mistake. Even if someone else wants to coerce, intimidate, or oppress you, choices and options are available. I'll give you a transparent look at what I learned the tragic way, next.

UNPACKING YOUR SHOEBOX

1. The shoebox effect does not always come in the form of boxes, and they sometimes hold items besides shoes. Physically, they can formerly house food, beverages, appliances, and even cigars. They can look like boxes, bags, barrels, or drawers. Emotional boxes can appear differently from mental or spiritual ones. What do your boxes look like? _____

   _____

   _____

   _____

   _____

   _____

The Shoebox Sherpa's Points to Ponder

- Shoeboxes can be held in your heart, mind, spirit, or hands.

- Emotional shoeboxes are hidden in our hearts.

- Mental shoeboxes are stored in our brains.

- Spiritual shoeboxes are captive in our souls.

- Physical shoeboxes are housed in places for safekeeping.

2. Do you have a physical shoebox or a metaphorical shoebox that you hide things in? _____

CHAPTER TWO

PLEASE SIGN HERE

C hoices. We're told we have them in any situation, but there are some circumstances that can make us believe we are helpless. Can you recall times you've felt intimidated, coerced, or oppressed? More than once, it's happened to me.

The pain of Dreyfus's death disturbed the slumber of my demons, awakening them with an angry vengeance. Renewed and alert from their many years of rest, they came prepared to collect their denied justice.

A couple of nights after my precious pet died, I collapsed on the couch after an especially long day of advising financial investors and managing employees in my job as a bank vice-president. At home, I sniffled, dabbed my eyes, then leaned over to put the wadded-up tissue on the end table. The shoebox on the top shelf of my bookcase caught my attention. I'd moved it when I got home from the veterinarian's office and forgotten about it.

I walked over and pulled the shoebox down, placing it carefully on the ottoman in front of me. Though the box was free from the confines of my closet, my mind was still emotionally imprisoned from an event that had taken place years before. I believed I deserved a self-imposed sentence that I hadn't fully served yet. I'd felt that way for decades.

Occasionally, when I allowed myself, I daydreamed about her. Where was she? Did she know about me? Was she happy? Was she living the advantaged life I was promised? Had I done the right thing?

Where was my daughter—my beautiful innocent little baby? My mind took me back to November 1978.

Meeting Jessica

My body felt weak right after giving birth, but I gathered every bit of spiritual strength I could muster. I knew what I wanted. The only ones left in the delivery room were me, a nurse, and my freshly swaddled infant. I didn't even know its gender yet.

I glared at the nurse. "Let me see my baby."

Her pinched face gave me her answer. I did not like it.

Fearless, I pushed forward. "I *said,* let me see my baby."

Obviously just as determined, the nurse glowered right back at me. Her facial expression looked as uptight as her starched uniform. "Your doctor does not recommend it. It would be better for you if you didn't."

Only weeks before, Dr. Stanley had coldly said the same. "It would be better if you did not see your baby."

Little did I know that their desire to keep me separated from my child was for their own personal gain. Dr. Stanley was on a mission to take my baby. But I wasn't going to make it easy.

I leaned up on an elbow and struggled to see my child. I squinted my eyes and spoke to the nurse in the starched, white uniform, "This adoption will take place on my terms, not yours. Let me see my baby. Now!"

She avoided my icy stare, picked my infant up, and walked toward the door, mumbling on the way. "I'll see what I can do."

I listened to the disappearing *squeak, squeak, squeak* of her shoes as she moved out of sight and made her way down the corridor. I'd never felt so alone—or so angry.

A few minutes later, the nurse surprised me by re-entering the room with a tiny bundle wrapped in a pink blanket.

"A girl?" I asked, choking on the words.

Still stoic, the nurse simply said, "Yes, it's a girl," as she placed my daughter in my arms for the first and last time.

While I stared in awe at the beautiful little life I held, the nurse shifted from foot to foot, as if the tiled floor was burning her feet. "I'll give you a few moments alone," she said. She stopped at the door, hesitated, then looked back with an expression of reluctance on her face.

I removed the blanket gingerly, releasing my daughter's pudgy arms first, then exposing her sweet, little baby belly. I stroked her soft facial features with my fingers and leaned down to breathe in her precious scent. Though they had different fathers, I marveled at how much she looked like her older sister, Michele, my three-year-old, conceived with my ex-husband, Bill.

As infants, both of my girls were born with the same red faces and dark hair, and though their paternity differed, they shared nearly identical features. But there was one striking variation—the eyes looking at me from my newborn's face. I could not deny the resemblance. My daughter, Jessica, only minutes old, looked at me through his eyes. Roger's.

Jesse, my freshly chosen nickname for my daughter, murmured, breaking the spell those eyes could cast on me. I couldn't think about Roger now. After all, he had walked out on us. I squeezed my eyes to shut out the memory of our last night together, knowing now, that as much as I'd hoped and believed, he was not coming back for us after all.

I stared down at this beautiful child Roger and I had created together and kissed her lightly on the forehead. Then I closed my eyes and prayed.

Something warm grabbed me. I opened my eyes to see Jesse's tiny hand curled around my pinky finger. It was as if she felt the swirl of all my love, grief, and pain, and wanted to comfort me. The way she clutched me made me think of "pinky swear," like we were making a promise to one another—no matter where she went, no matter who parented her, no matter how many miles or minutes separated us, I would always be a part of her, and she a part of me. Nothing and no one could change that.

I heard the swish of the door opening. The uppity nurse walked in, followed by a young man pushing a wheelchair. The nurse still avoided eye contact, but briskly approached the bed, and without speaking, wrenched my child from me. A piece of my soul shattered in that moment. I instantly felt a cold numbness fill my veins.

The nurse stated sternly, "Gabe is here to take you to your room."

I did not acknowledge her or look in the direction of the man holding the chair. I obediently let him guide me into the seat. Without an exchange of words, he wheeled me out of the delivery room, the nurse followed behind carrying my child.

In the hallway, Gabe with me and the nurse with Jesse, moved in opposite directions. My daughter's cries were the only sound I heard as they echoed behind me. Her wailing seemed to intensify the further we grew apart. As we neared the elevator, I strained my ears to hear Jesse, but her screams were no longer audible. My heart began to race—I realized I would never hear my daughter cry again.

Reality Hit

The wheelchair bumped rudely into the elevator. The heavy metal door closed slowly, shutting off all connections to my baby. This little person who had been a part of my every move for the past nine months was suddenly gone. I felt like someone had cut off my oxygen—I could no longer breathe.

Seeming to come from a long distance, I heard a kind voice say, "Marcie? Are you all right? Hey, it's okay. It's all going to be okay."

For the first time, I looked up into the soft, compassionate face of the orderly.

Gabe said, "Let's get you into your room and get you settled. You'll feel much better."

Confused, I said, "My room? Where are we?" Then reality hit me. By moving me off of the maternity ward, away from the babies and my daughter, they were trying to pretend as if I'd just had a routine surgery, instead of giving birth to a part of myself. But this wasn't routine to me. I'd carried this human being under my heart.

As Gabe wheeled me into room 301, the impact of my decision slammed into my gut. The room felt vacant and cold, like the aloof doctor and nurse who'd just taken my child from me. I had no family, friends, or other well-wishers waiting and welcoming. There were no flowers or cards to brighten the stark space. Balloons and teddy bears didn't have my daughter's name on them.

It was the 1970s, when attitudes were slowly beginning to change, but unwed and single mothers were still ostracized by society. Many unwed mothers like me were either sent away or went into hiding.

In my case, I moved six hundred miles away from home. I'd already embarrassed my family by marrying and divorcing at a young age, and was now a single mom with a three-year-old toddler. I couldn't put them through this, too.

My older sister, Judy, was the only one who knew about and supported me through my second pregnancy, she'd even allowed me and my three-year-old, Michele, to live with her. But Judy couldn't take seeing my new daughter stripped away. She left the hospital when she heard Jesse's first cry. I didn't yet understand the full reasons why, but the pain of losing a child was more than my sister could bear.

Get a Hold of Yourself

I looked over at the chair beside my hospital bed. It was as empty as the vacuum in my womb and the barrenness in my spirit. By now, I knew being alone was not something you get used to.

I eased out of the wheelchair and stood on trembling legs. The orderly offered gentle support and assisted me to the side of the bed. As I sat, I thought of my mother and my chin quivered. Hot tears spilled onto my young face. I needed to feel Mommy's protective arms around me. I needed to feel the warmth of her skin against mine. I wanted to drink in her perfume and feel the security of her love. I shuddered as I thought of how life had already cheated me out of so much, and I was only twenty-two.

My parents' divorce had robbed me of my mother at only five years old, and now this. It wasn't fair. I'd been abandoned by my baby's father and forced by lack of resources and society's pressure to surrender my child to adoption. Why did a couple I'd never met get to know my daughter when I wouldn't have the chance? How would I ever heal and live a normal life?

My quiet tears turned into hysteria. "I want my mother. Where is my mother?" I wailed.

The orderly was clearly uncomfortable and had no idea how to console me. So, he didn't.

A few minutes later, a nurse I hadn't seen before entered the room. She pushed the orderly to the side and grabbed me by the shoulders, then shook me firmly. "Get a hold of yourself, young lady. You are disturbing the other patients. You need to put this behind you and forget it ever happened."

Stunned by her sharp words, I could not respond. Instead, I cried louder. I wanted to maneuver past her and run back to the nursery. But instead, I sat frozen on the edge of the bed, too afraid to move.

The nurse scowled at me and said tartly, "I'll give you something to help you sleep if you will just stop crying and be quiet."

I tried my best to control my sobs, but it was useless.

"Gabe, quiet her this instant," she demanded. "I'll be right back." She strode out quickly.

The orderly came and sank awkwardly beside me on the bed. I searched his eyes for anything that might ease my pain, but all I found was his own fear. Gabe gently placed his arms around me and said sweetly, "Go ahead and cry. Let it out. I'll stay with you. I am so sorry."

At last. I felt a touch of human compassion. I fell into his warm embrace, and let his comforting words cover me.

"It's okay. It's all going to be okay. Sh, go ahead and cry. Gabe's here," he said.

This simple act of kindness was the greatest gift I could have received in that moment. In gratitude, I smiled up at him weakly. I felt momentary relief—until the nurse returned with a needle.

She plunged the strong drug deep into the tissue of my arm, and almost instantly, I felt the effects. My mind began to drift away from the day's trauma. My eyes grew heavier and I welcomed the spreading warmth passing through my body. "Brahm's Lullaby" played softly in the background—either in the hospital or in the start of my dreams. *Another child has entered the world. I hope this baby gets teddy bears and balloons,* I thought. Then darkness enveloped me.

Moving On

The next morning, Dr. Stanley stopped by my room. "It may be hard for you now," he said, as he gazed at me over black, horn-rimmed glasses. "But in time, the pain will subside, and you will forget this ever happened."

Why does everyone want me to forget? I asked myself.

The doctor pushed his glasses higher up on his nose and continued, "It was the right choice, Marcie. The only one you could make. You understand that. Right?"

Who is he trying to convince? I sat motionlessly.

"This way you can move on with your life, go to college, and take care of that toddler you already have at home. Remember? We talked about this. And the baby will have everything you want for her, I promise."

Everything but her mother, I thought sourly.

"I am so proud of you," Dr. Stanley grinned at me.

All I could think was, *Proud? What the hell? I gave my child away. You're the one who approached me about adoption early in my pregnancy. You solicited and made arrangements to give my Jessica to the "perfect couple." You deemed them better parents than me, only because I am single and broke.*

I knew smaller living quarters and bank accounts didn't mean I had a smaller heart. I wanted my daughter, and the thought of another woman holding her and acting as if she was hers made me feel ill. But that was adoption. Dr. Stanley had signed me up for it.

I don't remember leaving the hospital or how I got home, only that my sister Judy tried to make things as normal as possible for me when I arrived at her house. Whatever normal was.

That night at dinner, I went through the motions, pushing chicken around my plate, trying to look as if I were eating.

Judy chirped about Thanksgiving, "Can you believe how fast it's gotten here?" Then she rattled off her menu and the guests she wanted to invite.

I tried to listen but couldn't concentrate on what my sister was saying. How could I think about the holidays when my entire world had been knocked off balance? How could I continue on with my life as if a tiny person I created but couldn't keep had never entered the world? How could I participate in casual conversations and act phony, as if I wasn't losing my mind? Then, the unthinkable happened.

I smiled.

A funny comment triggered it, nothing hysterical, just the kind of ordinary statement that makes you react without thinking. I immediately covered my mouth with my hand. *How dare you smile or laugh?* I chastised myself. *This is inappropriate—like laughing at a funeral.* In my grief, my smile felt like I was betraying my child.

I quickly excused myself from the dinner table and ran to my room, crying. I threw myself on the bed, my heart splintering into thousands of pieces.

How was I supposed to live like Jesse didn't exist? How was I supposed to look for a job and make a home for my toddler, while a piece of our family was missing? How could I move back into mommy-mode, taking care of Michele, when I couldn't take care of Jesse? Would I ever be able to make my oldest daughter her favorite breakfast and read her a story without falling apart? It felt impossible. My sadness turned to anger.

I cursed Dr. Stanley for dismissing my trauma as nothing. How dare he call his manipulation a selfless gift? This was nothing of the sort. Giving gifts should include a sense of joy and happiness, but there was nothing joyful in what I'd felt cornered to do.

I had no guidance on how to process my emotions. I was given no instructions with my hospital discharge papers. I didn't get a manual titled, *How to Move on with Your Life After You've Given a Part of Yourself Away.* There were no emergency directions labeled: *In case of mental breakdown, follow steps one, two, and three.* Instead, I was essentially told, "Please sign here and hand me your infant."

After my sobs reduced to hiccups, I slowly crawled off the bed and took a position I hadn't been in since I was a small child. I dropped to my knees, bowed my head and prayed.

> *God,*
>
> *Will you please watch over my daughter? Keep her safe. Let her know I love her and help her to grow up happy. And Lord, if it's okay, could you show her how to forgive me someday? I know I don't deserve it, but I thank you.*

I felt an immediate calmness and sense of serenity come over me. The searing pain hadn't left, and I realized it never would. I could accept that. Like one of my legs, it was now a part of me—forever joined. I could either let it cause me to limp or propel me forward. So, I made a decision.

Desperately Seeking Peace

I parked my pain. If I could not make it stop, I would learn to control it. I would master it and train it into submission. I proclaimed dominance over my pain, telling myself I would never allow it to run my life. I stood up, walked to my nightstand, and grabbed my journal and the #2 pencil from inside the drawer. I thought of Jesse's father, Roger, and my dashed dreams of what I had imagined about our lives together. I jotted the date in the upper, right-hand corner, and I began to write.

Roger said, "I'm not ready to be a father, Marcie. I'm not the marrying kind. I can never give you what you want."

I know his words were spoken in truth, yet not meant to be unkind. But they haunt me. Why couldn't he want me and our child?

Fresh tears ran off my cheeks—thinking of Roger hurt too much. The peace I'd felt only moments before had already slipped out of my grasp, and I couldn't find a way to seize it again. For some reason, I didn't consider praying once more.

I threw the journal and pencil down and bolted for my suitcase, still packed from my hospital stay. Gabe, the orderly who had shown me compassion, had given me a book before I left and told me about a particular message inside. I clicked the latch on my luggage and dug through the contents. Pushing my slippers to the side, I found what I was searching for.

I leafed through the pages of *The Prophet*, by Kahlil Gibran, until I located the passage Gabe had underlined, a poem titled, "On Children." I read and re-read the poem, desperately seeking some hidden message, but found none. In the hospital, Gabe told me this poem had offered him a sense of peace, but though I was desperate to calm my weary soul, I found none of the peace Gabe described.

I walked back to the bed where I'd thrown my journal down and picked it back up. I stared at it and looked at the date. Then I circled the word November as I thought, *It's such a cold, dark month. And this is the coldest and darkest time in my life.*

I didn't know Novembers could last for years.

I wish I'd better understood the choices we have and the power they hold when I was talked into relinquishing my daughter. As much as I'd like, I can't go back in time, but what I can do is hopefully save others from years of torment like I experienced. Am I speaking to you?

If I could tell my younger self anything, it would be what I want to tell you now. "Refuse to let anyone intimidate, coerce, or oppress you.

Fight hard for what you want and need. Resolve not to give up. Don't let the shoebox effect steal years from your life."

In the next chapter, I'll share some ways I both succeeded and failed at acting with courage. I want you to learn from my mistakes and draw inspiration from my wins.

UNPACKING YOUR SHOEBOX

The Shoebox Sherpa's Points to Ponder

• Just because someone else pressures you does not mean you have no choice.

• When you feel helpless, try to look at your situation objectively. If this was happening to a stranger, what kind of advice would you offer them? What can you do to take that advice yourself?

• Give yourself permission to fight for what you want and need.

• Pray for peace, not only when you are desperate, but on a regular basis.

1. Has someone else ever pressured, intimidated, or coerced you into stuffing contents (physically, emotionally, mentally, or spiritually) into a real or metaphorical box?

_____

_____

_____

_____

_____

2. Do you have a single shoebox or multiples? _____

CHAPTER THREE

A BOX IS BORN

Courage comes in many forms. It's even possible to act courageously while not recognizing it as doing a gutsy thing. Other times, simply breathing is the bravest choice we can make. Too often, we discount the tiny steps we take that accumulate and lead to progress. Have you ever felt like you were getting nowhere in the moment, only to look back later and see how small decisions moved you forward?

As I continue sharing the dramatic events that led to my understanding of the shoebox effect, I hope you feel encouraged and affirmed. No matter what you are dealing with today, even if you only make one minuscule decision, you have done something progressive. I didn't realize it at the time, but my fresh grief over Dreyfus's death gave me the grit to consciously recall the details of another loss. It didn't seem like much of a move while it happened, but I would later realize I had taken a giant leap in courage.

It had been a whole week since I lost Dreyfus. My rediscovered shoebox sat poised on the living room ottoman. I'd walked around it for days, trying to ignore its incessant call.

To anyone else, it was just an old, nondescript box, beat up and faded, secured with a tattered yellow ribbon. I'm sure anyone else would have found it uninteresting, but to me it contained compelling contents. Family secrets, lies, shame, heartbreak, and loss were concealed within this thin cardboard vault. If opened, I feared it would unleash all the pain I'd parked inside, and perhaps, weaken the control

I'd worked so hard to master. I desperately needed to power through to fulfill my desire for peace—or so I thought.

I circled my earth-toned ottoman, as if I expected the shoebox to shape-shift and come to life. I gulped Chianti from my glass with each step. I needed liquid courage. The thundering silence in my living room caused the whispers in my mind to echo more loudly.

The box summoned. *Open me. It's been too long since you looked inside. It's no accident that Dreyfus knocked me over.*

Was it the wine or the shoebox beckoning me? And why was I scared of a little, bitty piece of cardboard?

Ghosts of Guilt and Shame

I thought about the last time I'd allowed myself to handle the box, twenty-eight years prior, in November 1979—on my daughter Jesse's first birthday.

Recalling that painful experience reminded me of a scene right out of the iconic sci-fi flick, *Poltergeist*[2]. I identified with the mother in the movie, when she sees the image of her daughter inside the TV. I thought it ironic that the spirits of both our little girls were tied to a box.

Like the mother, I fought emotions that nearly paralyzed me. I tried to make sense of the surreal situation I was put in, and I desperately wanted to find a way to get my child back. But I wasn't able to free my little girl in 1979. Instead, I ended up trying to drown my pain in a fifth of Southern Comfort. Besides giving myself a hangover, all I really accomplished was adding more ghosts of guilt and shame to the memories that already haunted me. Even whiskey hadn't helped me gather the courage to take the lid off my shoebox that night.

Forcing my mind out of 1979 and back to 2007, I cringed, both at the recollections, and the fear of opening my shoebox now. I willed my restless steps to carry me to the couch. I sat and put my glass of Chianti down. As I reached for the fading, yellow ribbon, I noticed

2 https://www.imdb.com/title/tt0084516/

the tremble in my fingers. I'd seen that tremble before—when I filled the box with items and tied the bow around it the first time.

November Rain

In 1978, the dark, cold, November night I'd come home from the hospital, after I'd fled the supper table, I picked up my journal and pencil again. Only now, it was as if something had possessed me and was writing instead. The pencil took over.

I poured out all of the emotions I felt, everything that made me believe I was a failure and made me unforgivable. I wrote for about an hour. When I finished, a small dent in my finger and cramped hand left evidence of my intensive grip on the pencil. But as I reviewed the results, I realized I'd said a final farewell to the child who would forever hold a part of my heart. My words to her came in the form of a poem. I carefully tore the poem out of the journal and read it to myself out loud.

November Rain

Our nine-month journey started
the first day that I found,
I carried you within me,
my love for you abound.
I knew I couldn't keep you,
for you weren't mine to keep,
You deserved a chance at life,
my love for you ran deep.
Each day you grew inside me,
my heart would swell with pride,
To know that you would someday be,
the light in someone's eyes.
I'd lay awake at night and dream,
of birthdays that I'd miss,

First steps, a smile, your laugh or cry,
> *your happiness I wished.*
One day you'll learn the story,
> *one day you'll understand why,*
The sacrifice I made for you,
> *will open up your eyes.*
So, I will carry all the pain,
> *the loss is mine to bear,*
My sweet, sweet child enjoy your life,
> *and know that I did care.*
I never will forget you,
> *in my heart you will remain,*
The tears I cry for you this day,
> *fall like November rain.*

As I lay the page down, a creeping hysteria crawled from my gut toward my throat. I thought about the trusted professionals who had said, "Move on with your life. Act as if you haven't given birth. You will forget this in time."

Ironically, their pressures to surrender my child had started me on a painful spiral. But now, I considered their advice to set my feelings aside, and took the first step toward willing my painful emotions into retreat. My spirit of fear was replaced by a wisp of empowerment—it gave me an idea.

Near My Heart

I walked to the closet and rifled around until I found what I was looking for. I grabbed the box, opened the lid, pulled the tissue aside, and carelessly tossed my new shoes onto the floor. I carried the shoebox to the bed and gathered items that held bittersweet value for me.

I tenderly placed *The Prophet,* given to me by Gabe the orderly, inside. I followed with my journal, along with photos of Roger and me, and the poem I'd just written. I sadly realized I had no baby bracelet or pictures of Jessica, but I needed some remembrance of her and our connection. Suddenly it came to me, I knew what to include.

In my suitcase, I found it. I lifted the maternity shirt out. I had worn the top to the hospital only two days before, when Jessica still lay beneath it, and rested near my heart.

I brought the garment to my face, closed my eyes, and took a long draw of its scent. Then I picked up a pair of scissors and cut a corner of fabric from near the hem. I placed it delicately inside the shoebox among the other mementos and shut the lid. Finally, I took a yellow ribbon I'd saved from a recent birthday gift and wrapped it around the box, then tied it tight.

I clutched the box to my chest as if it was gold, walked silently back to the closet, and placed it on the upper shelf. With extreme intentionality, I buried my most hurtful memories in that hidden place, one where my secrets would remain frozen in time, untouched for years. I thought I'd found a way to heal—a way to contain my demons. But twenty-nine years later, they still chased me.

Facing Demons and Lost Loves

Although I had built a successful life by most standards, it was all a facade. By September 2007, I'd simply become the consummate actress, skillfully hiding my truth, even from me. The oppressive sadness I felt refused to allow me relief.

At this stage, I was clueless and unconnected to anyone within the adoption community. I didn't even know there was such a group. Social media was in its infancy, texting was just becoming a thing, online banking and payments were barely trusted, and generally, adoption details were mainly spoken of in whispers—if at all.

Until then, I had tried to avoid the topic of adoption or anything that might make me think about it. I had no interest in the growing appeal for rare reunion stories, where missing family members found each other. I was still living in a lie. I was running from my truth.

But a week after losing Dreyfus, I began to think differently. Already at a crossroad in my life, I tried to clutch my long-held belief that no good could ever come from digging into the past. However, thanks to Dreyfus, my shoebox had come looking for me. Stirred memories refused to allow me to hide behind my comfortable facade for even one moment more.

I stared at the box and cursed myself for the 3,647th time. *How were you so naïve? Did you really believe a little shoebox filled with mementos would bring you healing?*

Thinking about the circumstances from my past, I thought, *They may have coerced me into surrendering my child, but no amount of influence can make me surrender my heart.*

Logically, I knew you couldn't hide from what haunts you, so I wondered, *Why can't I just pull the lid off the box and exorcise those secrets?*

Acutely aware of the suffering this Pandora's Box could unleash, I considered what might happen when I released all of the pain represented by the items inside. I braced myself for the *Poltergeist* that was sure to emerge. Somehow, I needed to face my demons.

I reminded myself, *You are no longer a young person, easily preyed upon. You are now a brave, independent, grown woman of fifty-two who knows her own mind. You are no longer innocent and naïve, but strong and assertive. You've learned resilience. You've conquered disappointment many times and turned failure into success. You know how to respond to difficult challenges. Life experience is your weapon against old demons.*

Sure, it's going to be tough at times, but you've longed for, even ached, to reclaim your missing past. No matter the outcome, you are equipped to deal with whatever waits ahead.

I walked to my fireplace and gazed at my reflection in the gold-framed mirror hung above the mantle. I searched for a hint of the face of my youth. Closing my eyes, I recalled the innocence and free spirit of the younger me.

I felt the warmth of a presence. I heard a voice I hadn't heard in years.

Open it, Marcie, the voice said in my mind.

Roger, the father of my surrendered child, was like our shared daughter—an unfinished chapter I wanted to go back and complete. It was if my lost loves were both beckoning me, "We're waiting for you."

When no one else was around, I sometimes allowed myself the indulgence of remembering the scent of Roger's cologne. I relived our passion. I'd never forgotten the exhilaration of falling in love. But, like Jesse, Roger was ripped away from me. The memories of my daughter and her father were woven together. The two of them were locked in my heart forever—the tangible reminders kept locked away inside my shoebox.

It took twenty-eight years, but on a cool, crisp evening in the fall of 2007, I bravely broke through my fear and picked up my tattered box. As I gingerly slipped the aging ribbon off, my eyes drifted to the corner of my living room, landing on Dreyfus's pet bed. It was empty, except for his collar.

Once again, fresh grief washed over me. My sweet, sweet golden. Dreyfus was finally free of his pain—and his last gift to me was to try to free me from mine.

"I miss you, buddy" I said softly, brushing a solitary tear from my cheek.

Holding my breath, I lifted the lid off my box. Steeling myself, I paused. The screaming demons I'd envisioned were not there. To my surprise, I instead discovered the sounds and smells of the hot summer of 1973. Opening the box roused the details that took me back to the very first day I laid eyes on Roger Roth.

Captivated

The first couple of months after high school graduation, I focused on breaking out of my rule-restricted home. Anxious to live a life free from the militant influence of my daddy, I seized my independence. I thought, *This is the life. No one can tell me no, now.*

Much too naïve and inexperienced, and with no direction, I began to flounder right away. After a short trip to Indianapolis to visit my mother and new stepfather, I bought a bus ticket and headed for Pennsylvania. I was ready to spend some quality time at the home of my married sister, Judy.

The Greyhound bus finally made its way to Reading, Pennsylvania, a short drive from Judy's home in Adamstown. As our driver, Tony, skillfully maneuvered through the bustling terminal, I breathed a sigh of relief.

With each passing mile of the fourteen-hour journey, I had felt a piece of the legalistic, authoritative voices I'd known my whole life, drifting away. During the long drive, I distracted myself among the pages of my paperback copy of Mario Puzo's *The Godfather*. Mile-by-mile, chapter-by-chapter, I felt even more liberated.

I spied Judy and my niece, MaryBeth, and sprang from my seat. My older sister represented home.

A couple of days later, after I'd settled in, Judy offered to take me to the Adamstown public pool. We made the short walk from her house on Main Street.

We could already hear the music blasting from a nearby jukebox as we made our way through the entrance turnstile. The scent of swimming pool chlorine and sun tan lotion filled my nostrils. I smiled. I so loved the water, and it had been weeks since I had been swimming.

The place was packed with people ready to escape the heat and cool off. Judy and I searched for a place to spread out our beach towels. I was scanning the crowd when I first laid eyes on him.

He leaned lazily against the fence, and I took my time absorbing every inch of him. His open shirt and white shorts made the most of his tan, long, muscular legs. The sun caused the hint of silver in his dark hair to glint. Silver? How could that be? He didn't look old enough for salt in his pepper-colored hair.

The woman he was talking to laughed at something he said, and when he smiled back at her, white teeth gleamed almost as brightly as his enormous blue eyes. I could tell she was in love with him by the way she seemed to see only him. I didn't blame her. He certainly was eye candy.

Judy nudged my calf, "What are you staring at?"

I turned in the direction of my sister. She had already placed her towel down and was beginning to cover herself in suntan lotion. I watched her push short, blonde bangs off her face with her sunglasses while she continued covering herself in Coppertone.

"Who is that, Jute?" I said, returning my stare to the gorgeous man.

"Who?" she stopped slathering and followed the direction of my eyes. Then she groaned. "Oh, Marcie. That's Roger Roth. He's the biggest ladies' man in town."

Ignoring her comment and continuing to stare, I said, "Is he married?" My heart pounded while I waited for my sister's answer. *Please, let that not be his wife,* I thought.

"Are you kidding? No way. But . . ." Judy jerked her chin toward Roger's trim, lady friend in the flattering red swim suit, "she sure is."

I turned my attention to the woman with the dark hair twisted on top of her head. She looked as if she were much older than Roger. And she was openly flirting with him. I watched her finger a small silver necklace, fingernails painted a bright red that matched her toes. She had a nice little figure, but I didn't think she was much of a beauty. And true to my sister's words, a gold band glittered on her left hand.

An announcement came over the PA system. "Phone call for Delores Fritz, you have a phone call. Please come to the front desk."

With one last flirty glance at Roger, the woman slung her sheer white cover over her bare shoulders. Leaning in to whisper a parting remark to him, she disappeared into the crowd.

"Will you please sit down?" Judy's voice tore me away from the man who had captivated my attention. My sister picked up her novel. "I thought we were here to sun ourselves. Remember?"

I reluctantly smoothed out my beach towel. But before I sat beside Judy, I glanced toward the fence once more—and found myself staring straight into those amazing blue eyes. Entranced, I couldn't blink or pull away.

Roger eyed me up and down while sweat prickled between my small breasts. His stare made me feel naked and acutely aware of my appearance. At eighteen, I was tall, tanned, and skinny—the opposite of the woman he was with. My blonde hair, parted straight down the middle, hung well past my shoulders. My black bikini clung to my body and his quirked brow told me he approved. In spite of the heat, I felt myself flush from his intense stare.

My sister's voice broke into my thoughts. "Better watch yourself," she warned before flipping a page in her novel.

I turned in her direction. "Might help if I knew why," I said, trying to pretend innocence.

"He's way too experienced for you, Marcie. Out of your league."

One Small Act

I had very little experience with men. I'd dated plenty of boys in high school, but I made it all the way to my senior year before I lost my virginity, just weeks shy of my eighteenth birthday. It was painful and awful, but I had finally 'done it' and joined my girlfriends who giggled during late night slumber parties. I had feared being on the receiving end of the whispers about girls who left school suddenly and "went away." So, I waited longer than some of my friends.

I married Bill several months later but wasn't in love. Boredom drew me to him in the first place, and now I was stuck in our union. It felt more like a transaction than a relationship. I felt empty. My frustration consumed me.

Delores's voice suddenly filled the air. I could hear her as clearly as if I'd stood next to her and the hunk who made me forget I'd ever said, "I do."

"Roger," she gushed. "I've been gone five minutes and you're already checking out the girls. You're such a bad boy!" Her sugary, sweet giggle made me feel nauseous.

I watched as he said something that made her smile, and put his arm around her tiny waist, steering her off in another direction. But he took a last look over his shoulder before guiding her away. He flashed his brilliant, white smile my way and winked. Our brief encounter would redirect the entirety of the rest of my life, though we wouldn't see each other again for some time.

Three years later, I spotted Roger in town. Coming out of a grocery store, I watched his tall, handsome figure saunter right past me. Wondering if he had married, I checked out his left hand in search of a gold band. His ring finger was still bare. I looked down at my own hand, void of a wedding ring.

After that, I found myself thinking of Roger often. He hadn't yet taken me to the shoebox effect, where I shunned the slightest thought of him, in hopes of escaping unimaginable pain. But it didn't work.

Avoidance never accomplishes what we hope. We can lose years of our lives to drained time, energy, and even money, when we attempt to hide from painful memories or an unfulfilled past. Though our instincts tell us the opposite, gathering courage and honestly dealing with what we've tried to ignore is the secret to lasting freedom from what haunts us. This is true even when our greatest pain comes from choices and situations we brought upon ourselves.

In the next chapter, I'll bare my soul and tell you how unlocking desire ended up placing me in an emotional prison. I hope sharing the transparency of my mistakes will save you from starting or continuing your own shoebox effect.

UNPACKING YOUR SHOEBOX

The Shoebox Sherpa's Points to Ponder

- Avoiding the contents of your shoebox will not make them go away.

- The longer a shoebox is ignored, the harder it becomes to deal with its contents.

- Bravely telling just one safe person about the contents of your "shoebox" can begin loosening the chains keeping you imprisoned by a painful past.

- Writing down how you feel is a healthy way to express emotions and get yourself through some very hard moments.

1. What are you afraid will get you if you face the contents of your forgotten shoeboxes?

   _____

   _____

   _____

   _____

2. Where do you store your shoebox(s) to avoid facing the contents—in plain sight or in a space you rarely visit? _____

   _____

   _____

   _____

CHAPTER FOUR

UNLOCKING DESIRE

Desire, longing, passion—none of these words are inherently bad. These are the emotions that can drive us to act when we would otherwise stay stagnant. I'd hate to live in a boring world where our hearts didn't thump and our pulses didn't race at the thought of something or someone that excited us, wouldn't you?

But attractions, cravings, and temptations for the unhealthy or unethical, though they feel good in the moment, can lead to much hurt later on. Have you ever given in to something you wanted and then paid a steep price later?

Because I cannot imagine not having the blessing of my children and grandchildren, I wouldn't change many of my past decisions. But if I could somehow do a few things differently, to protect all of us from preventable pain, I'd go back in time without hesitation. If only I'd had the benefit of wisdom when things escalated in 1977.

I found my sister shrouded in a cloud of Aqua Net. She was just putting the finishing touches on her hair when I entered the room.

"Want me to do yours?" Judy asked for the thousandth time in my life.

Ever since I could remember, my sister had cared for my hair. Judy wanted to braid it, twist it, curl it, or cut it. I always thought she missed her calling in life—she should have had her own salon.

I watched Judy as she teased her short blonde tresses with a comb, then painted a deep shade of coral lipstick on her lips. Her simple, white summer shift was an elegant choice and set her violet-blue eyes off—they were a matched set to our mother's. Alike in many ways, sometimes strangers mistook Mom and Judy for sisters.

Feeling oddly light-hearted in contrast with the heavy state of my relationship with Bill, I smiled at Judy, "No, not today," I said. "I think I'll leave it down for tonight."

"Suit yourself." Grabbing my hand in hers, Judy pulled me toward the door. "Come on, let's go downstairs and see what Gary is up to."

We followed the country melody trailing up the staircase and found Judy's husband icing beer and soft drinks in green Coleman coolers scattered around the backyard. Conway Twitty's voice blared from the radio. My sister rolled her eyes. She hated Conway Twitty's music.

Judy and I covered the picnic tables with red and white checkered tablecloths, then added matching cloth napkins and small vases adorned with daisies. Besides looks, my sister had inherited our mother's sense of style and love for classy entertainment touches. With Judy, plastic tablecloths weren't used, and you didn't wear cut-offs. No hamburgers and hotdogs were served. Instead, Judy offered steak and salad, with drinks poured into real glasses. And she dressed like she was doing a photo shoot with *Better Homes & Gardens*.

That night, the tables looked great. No detail had been overlooked. Gary was lighting the charcoal when the first guests began to arrive. My job was to welcome everyone at the front door and escort them to the back. The air felt electric, as if something inside me knew what was about to happen.

Remembering

While I waited to greet people in the living room, I looked through my sister's records, finding a 45 rpm that had belonged to our mother. My mind pulled up a memory of one of my rare weekend visits with Mommy. I must have been eleven or twelve. I could still see her swaying and singing to the sounds of Sandy Posey's "Born A Woman."

Lifting the lid off the stereo console, I gingerly placed the 45 on the turntable, twisted the knob, and turned up the volume. Posey's lyrics spoke to my unsatisfied soul. It seemed obvious that Sandy Posey understood a woman's plight. Filled with emotion, I identified with her words. Her song said that a woman's place is under a man's thumb, regardless of whether she had money or not, or whether she was brilliant or dumb. I felt Posey's pain when she said a woman was born to be hurt, lied to, and treated like dirt. As an adult woman listening to the words for the first time, I realized the lyrics were about a woman's oppression by a man.

As a child, I was always too enamored by my mother's movie star features and her ability to belt out Sandy Posey better than Sandy Posey to think about the song's meaning. Now I wondered about my mom, *Did she truly feel that way about men? How did she feel about my father?*

I never understood anything about my parents' marriage. It had been a taboo topic, never discussed by either of them—hidden—their deep, dark secret. Like missed crumbs under a kitchen rug waiting to be swept away, their relationship was not open for discussion.

As the last of Sandy Posey's melancholy refrain floated away, I poured myself a glass of wine. I wanted to hear her lyrics one more time, but before I could take a drink or place the needle on the record, the doorbell rang. I opened the door, then immediately stepped back. I couldn't believe who was standing in front of me.

How many times had I dreamed about Roger's sky-blue eyes?

Stammering, I started to introduce myself, but he interrupted.

Roger brushed against me as he moved himself inside. "You're Marcie, right? Judy's sister? I'm Roger. Gary invited me."

"Hello." I hated how weak my voice sounded. I blurted, "Yes, I remember you," but immediately regretted telling on myself.

Roger raised his brow, and a faraway look came over him. Suddenly, his expression widened, and he snapped his fingers, "The pool? That's right, I remember. We saw each other at the pool one day, right?"

I couldn't believe it. Three years was a long time. "I was there with my sister." A surge of excitement made my pulse thump. "Can I get you something? Would you like a drink?"

"A beer would be fine," he said, revealing his brilliant white smile.

I led him into the kitchen. Removing the cap and handing him the bottle, I watched as he took a drink of the amber ale. I soaked him in. He smelled heavenly.

After he'd finished off half of his beer, Roger held the door open for me and we made our way outside.

My brother-in-law approached with an outstretched hand. "Roger. Glad you could join us. I see you've met my sister-in-law already." Winking at Roger, he continued, "Now you need to be careful, she's married, you know."

"So, you told me," Roger said. But he wasn't looking at Gary. His stare went clean through me. I could tell that my marriage, whether good or bad, was just a detail to him. If he was interested, nothing would get in his way—and I wanted him to be interested.

Gary led Roger away and introduced him to some of his co-workers who were gathered by the grill. While they walked, Roger glanced back over his shoulder toward me. He gave me a wink, just as he had that day by the pool. The surge in my belly felt exactly as it had three years earlier.

Judy called me over to join her and some of the wives by the tables. I overheard one of the women ask my sister who he was. By her facial expression, Judy seemed irritated by Roger's presence. It was obvious she did not know he was coming.

"Better keep that handsome thing away from your little sister," one of the women joked.

"Mmmm, if I wasn't married," another said.

"How do you know him, Judy?" a trim redhead inquired.

I listened and watched, downing my glass of wine. I quickly poured another, intrigued when my sister joined the conversation. The women huddled their heads together like gossiping schoolgirls, occasionally looking around, as if they were protecting some secret. Thankfully, they couldn't read my mind.

Feeling Bold

I was not a seasoned drinker, so the wine immediately went to my head, spreading a warm glow throughout my body. By the time Judy called everyone to the tables for dinner, I felt an unfamiliar sense of boldness. Guests were selecting their places to sit, so I walked right up to Roger and flashed him my own dazzling smile. "Sit with me?" I said, openly flirting with him. He needed little encouragement.

Ignoring stares, we made our way to a table occupied by four others, now making us a party of six. We sat far away from my sister and Gary.

I'd barely sat down, when Judy came up behind me and with grit in her voice, said, "Can you help me in the kitchen?"

As soon as we were in the house and out of earshot from the others, she stopped abruptly. "What are you doing?"

Playing dumb, and embracing my new boldness, I said, "What? I'm not doing anything wrong. You just need to attend to your guests."

"Marcie, you're married," she spat.

"Really, Jute? Not you, too! You know I do not have a marriage, I have an agreement, plain and simple. Please, let me have a good time tonight. It's just dinner. Relax."

I turned to walk away, leaving Judy with her hands on her hips and a scowl on her face.

I was getting ready to open the door and step back outside when I heard Judy sigh. "Grab the butter out of the refrigerator, will ya?"

I considered ignoring my sister's request, but instead chose to comply.

Judy then handed me several breadbaskets, before opening the oven to retrieve the dinner rolls. "I just don't want you to get hurt." She filled the baskets in my hands with bread. "You're just asking for trouble."

I reassured her. "I'm fine, don't worry. Nothing's going to happen."

The way she cocked her head told me that my sister was not comforted.

We walked back outside, and I rejoined Roger, excited to be in his company again. We exchanged brief introductions with the people at our table. It was obvious he and I were the only ones who were not a couple.

The intoxicating mixture of wine, candles, and the beautiful night air made me feel as if Roger and I were transported somewhere else, away from the others. He leaned close several times and sighed discreetly, as he caught the faint scent of my perfume. When he secretly pressed the top of my thigh under the table, the heat of his hand sent a shockwave throughout my body. I was dizzy and craved more.

While I pretended to eat my dinner, pushing my steak and salad around the plate, I wondered. *What makes him so desirable? It's got to be something besides his good looks, although he does offer a nice view.*

I hung on his every word throughout the meal. An unfamiliar desire was filling my belly, making it easy to ignore my food.

After he finished eating, Roger excused himself and headed toward the house. The expression on his face said he wanted me to join him. I waited impatiently, hoping I'd given it an appropriate amount of time before I got up and followed.

When I got inside, Roger silently motioned, and we moved into the living room. He walked over to the stereo and thumbed through the eight tracks until he found something he liked. He popped the tape into a slot in the stereo console, flipped the toggle, and turned the knob. The smooth, bluesy sounds of Ray Charles softly filled the room. My heart raced as Roger approached.

Unlocked Desire

Without a word, Roger reached for my hand, pulling me to himself. I feared I might pass out. He caressed my hair and ran his soft fingers over my eyelids. We gently swayed with the music, our bodies moving in harmony. I wished the song and moment would never end.

He'd just leaned in and grazed his lips against my ear lobe, when the creak of the backdoor interrupted. I took a step back, my face flushed, my head spinning.

My sister was like a bloodhound let loose on a morning hunt. Noticing we were both missing from the table, she had wasted no time in politely excusing herself, so she could beeline her way to the house.

Before Judy had time to make it into the living room, Roger busied himself by pretending interest in my sister's large record and tape collection. I was unable to compose myself as quickly. When Judy entered the room, she immediately took in the flush I could feel on my face.

She placed her hands firmly on her hips. "We're choosing partners for cards." Jute glared at Roger. "Gary is looking for you."

Then she turned her attention on me with unmistakable disdain. My sister spat, "You stay here, I need your help."

Roger slipped from the living room, and I braced myself for whatever Judy was about to dish. Not one to mince words, she tore into me as soon as the screen door slapped against its frame.

I sighed and rolled my eyes while she ranted. Her words were nothing more to me than that, words. My mind was set.

Judy barked, "You will stay clear of Roger, do you hear me? We're going back out there to play cards and you're going to be *my* partner. Period. Understand?"

I refused to give her the satisfaction of a response.

Her face softened. "Now, stay beside me." Judy patted my hand, then led me to the door. We walked outside together.

I reluctantly obeyed her orders, but my spirit felt rebellious. I remained with Judy's group the rest of the evening and dutifully went through the motions. I served dessert and refilled glasses. I even feigned interest in the conversation between the women at our table. But when I thought no one else would notice, my eyes continuously scanned, seeking him, waiting for a glimpse of the man who had already mesmerized me.

As the party was ending, I watched Roger make his rounds, shaking hands and saying good night. He saved his final goodbye for Judy.

Though I kept a respectable distance, I could hear him thank my sister for having him. And just like that, he was gone. My heart sank. Roger had unlocked a desire inside me I hadn't known existed. And now that he'd unleashed it, there was no putting it back. I cared nothing about consequences—that would prove a big mistake.

It's hard to stuff passion back into a box once it's been released. If we succumb to strong emotions, we often act impulsively, not only hurting ourselves, but other people we care about as well. The shoebox effect starts long before we gather memorabilia to put inside—it begins with the decisions that create our memories.

If you can identify with any part of my story, and the emotions that led me to act without consideration for the damage I might do, I hope to protect you. I want you to know the time to prevent a consequence is before you end up in a tempting situation. Assess your emotional state when you have the ability to do so with a fair amount of objectivity. Don't think you can play with a seductive trap and get out before it snaps shut, breaking a part of you in the process. Early honesty can prevent a great deal of trauma.

Do you ever feel like something is missing—even if you can't identify exactly what that something is? When we embark on a quest to fill a void in our souls without weighing the costs for what we fill them with, we could end up paying for it the rest of our lives. As you'll discover next, I speak from the experience of hurting more than one person.

UNPACKING YOUR SHOEBOX

1. Has desire, longing, or passion ever gotten you in trouble?

_____

_____

_____

_____

_____

2. Do you find it more beneficial to plan your life or act spontaneously? What have been the outcomes from your decision-making patterns? _____

_____

_____

_____

_____

The Shoebox Sherpa's Points to Ponder

- Carefully consider whether you have any voids in your soul, creating a gnawing, emotional hunger inside.

- Be honest about not only what you feel, but why you think you feel it. Go back as far as you need-—weeks, months, or even decades—in order to identify origins of emotional weaknesses.

- When you feel lonely, isolated, or unappreciated, beware of the human ability to justify choices we would normally never consider.

- When temptation or seduction draws you, stop instantly. Give yourself a mere sixty seconds to play the situation out in your mind. Envision what the future will look like, not just for you, but for other people you care about, if you give in to the temptation.

CHAPTER FIVE

STICK IT TO THE MAN

I've never met a person who didn't have at least one secret. Some truths embarrass—some truths dredge up pain or fear—others can cause a great deal of anger. Pent-up anger often leads to decisions you can't take back. What I did to Bill started early in our relationship.

I did not want to marry him. As I walked down the aisle on the day of our wedding, I felt the pressure of my step-father's hand in mine. I disciplined my eyes to the front of the church, while my mind went wild.

Run, Marcie, run! You know this is a mistake. What are you waiting for, divine intervention? The signs are all pointing to the same answer.

I debated with myself. *I can't. I'll disappoint everyone. And my baby needs a father. I can't raise a child alone.*

I answered myself back. *Mom offered you a place to stay.*

The thought reminded me of the anger issues I had with my mother. A tidal wave of emotions surrounded my relationship with her, based on her abrupt departure in my young life. The trauma of losing her had left me wounded and scarred. But I couldn't deal with any of that right now—the bridal march was playing.

Ours was a marriage of necessity, by societal rules of 1973. Bill was my sister Judy's, brother-in-law. The only two things we had in common were our ages and our interest in riding horses. Bill spoke softly with a heavy Dutch accent, and often sounded as if he were mumbling. His seriousness bored me, though I appreciated his intelligence and quick wit. By the age of nineteen, I'd been married for almost a year and had a little girl.

I didn't understand who I was or what I wanted to do with my life. I was conditioned to just go along with the decisions others made for me.

Bill soon developed a habit I hated. Any time I mentioned making any improvements, such as saying I'd like to go to college or that it would be nice to get our own place, he resisted. With a monotone voice and little emotion, he often droned, "You're such a spoiled brat, Marcie."

But his efforts to suppress me and my desire for more just made me angrier and more stubborn. So, I developed my own unsavory habit. Trying to get him to show any emotional response, I would deliberately try to fight. No matter how hard I pushed, I could not get him to engage and react.

As my fury built with each passing day, I felt lonelier and more isolated. I began to take my frustrations out on everyone around me. An emptiness filled my soul with an unbearable ache and longing—for what, I didn't know. It made me vulnerable.

A Surprising Call

On a sweltering, lazy Saturday morning a week after the barbecue, I planned to sleep in as long as possible. I wanted to take advantage of the solitude while Bill and our daughter, Michele, were away at his family farm for the weekend. But the loud ringing of my downstairs telephone blew my plans. Sweating and irritated, I ran down the steps to answer it, swearing on the way.

I yelled at my absent husband as I rushed down the stairs, "Bill! Why can't you put an upstairs extension in?"

Bill's typical, unemotional, no-nonsense response sounded in my head. "Never had it growing up. Don't need it now. When you don't have it, you don't miss it. It's just like air conditioning, it's a waste of money. Your father just spoiled you."

STICK IT TO THE MAN 55

Even though Bill was not in the house, I shouted at him one more time before I picked up the phone. "Daddy didn't spoil me. He just wanted to make sure his family was comfortable, like normal people."

I hurried to pick up the receiver before the line went dead and answered sharply. "Hello."

A deep, alluring voice said, "Marcie? Hi, it's Roger."

I forgot to breathe for a moment. When I realized, I quickly sucked in air and stammered as I tried to keep the surprise out of my voice, "Hi. Good morning." Then I thought, *How did he get my number?*

"I'm so sorry if I woke you," Roger said smoothly.

"No problem," I said. "What's up? How are you?"

"Great, thanks. And you?"

Other than reliving last Saturday night over and over again in my head, I'm fine, I thought. But I said, "Besides being miserable from the heat, I'm good."

"It's going to be another hot one today," Roger said. "Hey, I wanna ask you a favor."

Curious, I thought, *He wants something? I hope what he really wants is me.* But once again, I made sure my words did not mirror my thoughts. So, I said, "I'll help if I can. What do you need?"

"Do you have any plans this morning? I sold my truck yesterday and found a car I wanna buy. I was wondering if you could give me a lift to the bank over in Lancaster County so I can sign the loan papers."

I needed no encouragement. "Sure," I said enthusiastically. "I can do that, no problem. What time should I pick you up?"

"Is ten too early?"

"Not at all. I will pick you up then."

He gave me his address, then said, "Great, thanks."

I heard him hang up, but I lingered before I put the receiver down. Roger had just called me on that phone.

I wondered, *Why didn't he ask one of his friends or family?* But deep down, I suspected I knew the answer to my own question.

Glancing up at the clock, I smiled. Eight forty-five gave me plenty of time. I sang on my way to the shower.

A Fast Move

Pulling up in front of his house an hour later, I glanced in the rearview mirror, checking my appearance one last time before blowing the horn. I had chosen my outfit carefully. I decided on a short summer skirt with mid-drift top that tied in the front with a tank underneath and no bra.

He bounded down his front steps and smiled.

He's so handsome, I thought. I wondered if he knew how much power he carried with those looks.

He slid into the passenger seat beside me and I tried to be discreet as I inhaled the scent of him.

"Well, you look nice." He winked at me.

I turned my eyes to the road ahead and shifted my Malibu into drive. I hoped he didn't see the blush warming my face. "So do you," I said.

Suddenly, I felt his hand on my knee. It reminded me of the same fast move he'd made last week at the barbecue.

I took my right hand off of the steering wheel and gently squeezed the top of his hand, then sighed. Three years after I'd first spotted him at the pool, we were finally alone. No stares, no judgment, no worry that someone might walk in. Roger and I, just the two of us.

We rode the back roads to the bank silently for the first ten minutes, without moving our hands. I was disappointed when I felt him slip his out and the warmth cool from my thigh.

Roger didn't acknowledge the removal of his hand. "I noticed you have a tape player. How about some music? You like Elvis?" he said.

Though I preferred rock and roll bands like Led Zeppelin, Grand Funk Railroad, the Who, the Doors, the Rolling Stones and the Beatles, I said, "Sure. Elvis is fine." I did have one Presley tape.

When I pulled into the bank parking lot, "Suspicious Minds" was playing in my eight-track.

"I won't be gone long," he said. I watched as his lean frame disappeared into the building.

I sang along with the tape while I waited, so I failed to hear Roger approach the car. When he opened the door, it startled me.

"Well, that's all taken care of," he said. "Thanks for doing this, Marcie. I really appreciate it."

I smiled. "No problem, glad to help," I said. What happened next was one of those unexpected moments I would relive for decades.

I pulled my car out of the parking lot in order to retrace our way to town. Traffic was light on the back road, so we hardly passed any cars. About five minutes into our drive, Roger suddenly reached for the steering wheel. I instinctively put my foot on the brake.

Roger seemed unaffected, and carefully steered my car off to the side of the road, then placed it into park. He turned to me without saying a word and cupped my face in both of his hands. He kissed me slowly. In his lips I felt both gentleness and passion. I had never experienced that level of emotion—and I didn't want it to stop.

He pulled back and our eyes locked. "I've wanted to do that ever since I saw you three years ago," he said.

My voice sounded hoarse in response. "Me too."

Roger reached for me and kissed me again. Only this time, it was deep and demanding, not the kiss of a boy. The way he probed left me breathless and dizzy—and craving more.

"I know you're married, and I don't care," he stated flatly. Then his voice became more determined. "Say you will go out with me. Tell me yes."

I didn't need to think about it. I had rehearsed a similar scene in my mind ever since he had winked at me over his shoulder that day at the pool. I locked my arms around his neck and looked deep into those searing eyes. "Yes, I will go out with you, Roger."

We made plans to meet the following Friday night, after Bill took Michele to the family farm for their customary weekend escape. They always left on Thursday night.

Keeping Secrets

All week, I counted the hours and minutes until I would see Roger again. The anticipation was so great, I feared I might give myself away. It helped to bury myself in house cleaning and mom duties. I took Michele to the park and pool multiple times. By the time Bill got home from work Thursday evening, I thought I might explode from the build-up.

When he finally showered, packed, and left for the country, I made the short drive to my sister's house. I hoped to sit on her porch and catch a glimpse of Roger driving by. But when I arrived, Judy kept me in the kitchen while she packed for their family camping trip.

"So, what are you doing this weekend while everyone is gone?" Judy dropped a bag of marshmallows into a cardboard box filled with canned goods.

"Not much," I lied. I looked down at my feet, too guilty to make eye contact.

Judy kept packing and moving, barely glancing at me.

Feeling the need to overexplain, I continued. "I'll probably just get some swimming in and try to keep cool. Or I may go out to dinner with Carol. She's off Saturday night."

"That's nice," my sister said offhandedly. "Hand me those paper plates and that silverware, will you?"

Judy accepted the eating utensils from my offered hands and chattered on. "I heard the restaurant is really good where she works. We should all go there some night when we get back."

I watched my busy sister intently. She seemed satisfied in her role of wife and mother, cook and housekeeper. Why couldn't I be more like her? Why did I feel so empty and angry? Why couldn't I settle and accept Bill's simple ways? What was it in me that knew I could never grow to love him?

I left Judy's house that evening feeling guilty about keeping my secret from her. I angrily wiped away my tears, as if I could erase what

I felt inside. Guilt and shame were familiar, they had been my companions since childhood.

The next morning, a beautiful ray of sunshine poured into my bedroom. I felt it was a sign that my date with Roger would be memorable. I was not disappointed—and the impact started early.

I stepped out my front door around 10:00 a.m. to go for a swim. I needed the distraction. On my fence railing lay a single red rose, and I could see a folded piece of paper beneath it. I picked up the note. It simply read, *Marcie, looking forward to tonight. Roger.*

I smiled at this thoughtful gesture. It made me want him all the more.

When he picked me up, he was right on time. I drank in the view of his tight Wranglers, light summer shirt, and cowboy boots.

I had sat on my sofa for over an hour before he arrived, listening to music and trying to relax. I made sure my legs were smoothly shaved and soft with lotion. I even used my special lemon cream rinse on my hair and waited until it was thoroughly dry before ironing it straight. My blonde locks had a natural wave and I was always fighting them. Tonight, they cooperated and let me win.

I sprayed the bathroom with Ambush perfume then walked through it, just like my sister had taught me. I didn't want the scent too strong, but I wanted it noticeable, so I added a bit behind both ears and knees.

My new black undergarments made me feel sexy and boosted my self-confidence. I mentally thanked my sister for talking me into purchasing them several weeks before. I stood sideways and viewed my body in the mirror, then smiled. Other than a few faint stretch marks, you could not tell I'd had a baby.

I fussed with my makeup until I rivaled the Revlon girls on TV. I wanted this night to be perfect—for him.

I'd never felt so anxious about going out on a date. I remembered what Judy had said. "He's out of your league."

Though it was only in my head, I suddenly felt my mother's presence in the room. I could sense her disappointment. Echoes of my mom's voice scolded me.

What are you doing, Marcie?

I imagined myself standing up to my mom. *What I should have done three years ago.*

The spirit of my mom said, *This is wrong, you're married.*

I slid into my tight Levi's, arguing while I hiked them into place. *But I don't love Bill. Marrying him was a mistake—we don't even sleep in the same bed anymore. Roger's the man I really want.* I jerked my freshly pressed blouse off of the ironing board, buttoned the shirt, shook my hair out one last time, and walked to the living room to wait.

I caught sight of the single, red rose on my kitchen table, and my blood pumped with fresh adrenalin. By the time I opened the door to greet the man who knocked, the juice in my veins flowed full throttle.

Surrender

He took me to a modified stock car race at the Reading Fairgrounds. Afterward, we walked the short distance from the track to a small bar and restaurant called the Do Drop Inn. Owned by three sisters, the place was covered in race memorabilia and was often frequented by many local drivers. Hats, jackets, tee shirts, and pictures covered the walls and hallways.

With one hand on the small of my back, Roger guided me across the room. As we walked, he exchanged greetings and nodded to some of the regulars. All of them smiled, except for a brunette sitting at the end of the bar.

Her eyes burrowed into me, and a look of despise covered her face. I could not understand why this woman I did not know would look at me with such contempt.

"Roger, who is that woman?" I asked after we finally got our seats in a booth away from the bar. "Do you know her?" I asked innocently.

He turned briefly in the direction I was pointing and said, "Nobody important." He motioned for the waitress to take our drink order.

I brushed it off. In my youth and lack of experience, I had no internal radar to alert me. I had no idea this was my first clue of what was to come.

Roger quickly dispelled any further questions by leaning over the table and gently tucking a short-stemmed, red carnation behind one of my ears. He was unpredictable and romantic. Sexy and alluring. Mysterious, yet bold. And I wanted him like I'd never wanted anything in my life.

It was after one o'clock in the morning when we finally made it back to my house. I did not question whether he was coming in. I turned the stereo on and looked for some records to play. As I shuffled through my vinyl albums, I felt his arms snake around me from behind. He turned me to face him and wasted no time.

"Now, where were we?" Roger said as he took my hand and placed it around his waist, pulling me into his embrace. "Ah, that's right," he said softly. "We were right here when your sister interrupted us."

I smiled as I felt his hand on the back of my neck, pulling me into a firm kiss. My head spun and every nerve in my body longed to make as much skin contact as possible. I returned his kiss with an urgent demand for more. The heat of his silent breath on my neck spread a warm glow throughout my young body as he backed me down onto my couch.

I surrendered.

Afterward, we went upstairs, where I surrendered again.

The last thing I remembered before falling asleep in his protective arms, was the shimmer of moonlight shining through my bedroom window. Its glow accented Roger's bronzed body. For the rest of my life, the moon's rays would remind me of our first night of passion. From that weekend on, my world revolved around the anticipation of our next tryst.

Mid-afternoon on Saturday, Roger left with a kiss and promise to call by Thursday. We planned to go out again on Friday night. I wondered how I could make it that long without seeing him. He'd only been gone minutes, and I'd already rewound my magical memories and replayed them multiple times.

Set Ups and Lies

Since Bill and Michele weren't coming back until Sunday morning, I busied myself with errands and an afternoon swim after Roger went home. I also joined my friend, Carol, for an early dinner, but back home by eight o'clock, I felt anxious and bored. So, I tried to watch a little TV. Eventually the exhaustion from my rendezvous with Roger and my time swimming under the hot afternoon sun hit me hard. I drifted off to sleep.

I was startled awake by the ringing telephone. I glanced at the clock as I got up to grab it—10:30 p.m. I had been asleep for over two hours. Still not fully alert, I stopped the shrill cry by picking up the receiver.

"Hello."

"Hi. It's me." Roger's voice washed over me, and a tingling began in my gut. Still not fully awake, I also felt confused. *Was it already Thursday?*

"I've been thinking about you all day," he said

"Me too. I had a great time," I said. "Where are you?"

"Home. I just thought I would give you a call. Wanted to hear your voice."

I melted. "Why don't you come over then?" I said boldly.

"Now?" he said. "Are you sure? It's late."

"Yes."

"I'll be there in twenty minutes," he said.

He made it in ten.

Looking back years later, I had to laugh at myself. I realized Roger was setting me up that night, pretending he had other motives for calling. He made me think it was my idea. It wouldn't be the last time he duped me. After that, lies started coming easier for me too.

One evening after I'd put Michele to bed, I told Bill, "I'm going down to Jute's then to the store."

Bill glanced at his watch, then back at me. "Can't it wait until tomorrow?"

I ignored his remark and grabbed my keys. Without looking at him, I said flatly, "We need milk. I'll be back in a little while."

Only one week into my affair with Roger and I was already looking for any excuse to get out of the house. When I showed up at my sister's, she read me quick. "Okay, give it up. What's going on with you? You don't show up here at nine o'clock for nothing. What's wrong?"

I wasn't ready to confess my feelings about Roger yet, but I did tell her, "I want to leave Bill and file for divorce. Will you help me?"

My sister didn't appear surprised, but she wasn't buying my entire story, either. "What's the rush? More to the point, what's your plan? You can't just walk out unless you are planning to move home to Indiana."

Unwilling to take the conversation further, I said, "I've got to go. I told Bill I was getting milk. I'll talk to you about it later." I felt Judy's scowl as I walked out her front door and headed back down Main Street. My real mission was to drive past Roger's house hoping to find him there.

A growing fear gripped my soul. *What are you doing?* I interrogated myself. I considered turning around toward home, but almost to Roger's house, I saw his silver Oldsmobile coming from the opposite direction. It pulled right up beside me, and I looked at the driver.

Roger smiled and signaled for me to wait a moment. He parked his car, hopped out, and took his front steps two at a time. He returned in moments holding a blue blanket.

Obsession

"Well, this is a nice surprise" he said. "Scoot over, let me drive."

I slid over to the passenger side. "Where are we going?" I asked anxiously. "I told Bill I was only going to the store."

He said nothing in response, but instead, looked at me with those mesmerizing eyes, grasped my hand, and kissed it. Then he pulled away from the curb.

Within three minutes we were making the short walk up a hill through the darkness, with only the evening moon as our guide. At nearly 10:00 p.m., the small park was deserted. The pine smelled comforting as, hand in hand, we walked deeper into the woods. Roger finally found a secluded spot under a tree and spread the blanket out on a bed of scented needles.

He spoke softly to me, taking my body to new heights of pleasure. My young heart soared when I heard him cry out, whispering my name in the still of the darkness.

I never made it to the store, and I lost all sense of time. In Roger's arms, I'd finally found a place where the emptiness disappeared. But home wasn't going away.

Within a few short weeks, I was no longer sleeping with my husband. The intensity of my affair accelerated to the point of obsession. One weekend away from Roger was all it took for me to implode.

I had not visited the farm with Bill for several months and his family started asking questions. The last thing I wanted was to hurt them, so when Bill begged me to go with him one weekend, I relented.

I tried to rationalize that I was doing it for them, but truthfully, I was doing it for me. I needed to buy a little more time. I had a toddler to consider. Though I wanted to leave my marriage, I couldn't just walk out with nowhere to go and no way to support my daughter. Bill would not be ignorant to that fact.

Since the night I came home empty-handed and late, Bill had began to question me about how I spent my weekends. While at the farm, he called several times each day and night to see if I was home. I was getting pressure from both directions.

Roger also began to call in the evenings throughout the week to see if I could get away. If I couldn't talk when he called, I would say the caller had the wrong number and hang up. My web of lies was thinning, and something was about to break.

At the farm with Bill, I made it through the first night, but not happily. I was sullen and quiet. The next day, I saddled up and went horseback riding by myself, choosing to stay away until nightfall. Apparently, I didn't stay gone long enough. As many times as I had rehearsed the end of my marriage, even I was surprised at my own cruelty when it happened.

Bill was gathered with his family in the living room, chatting after dinner. I marched in the room and blurted, "I can't do this anymore." I turned and walked out, packed my suitcase, got my daughter, and proceeded to leave. With a suitcase in one hand and Michele on my hip, Bill stopped me outside.

"What do you think you are doing?"

I simply said, "Leaving you. It's over."

His mouth was still open when I turned and walked to my car.

Putting the vehicle in gear, I felt empowered. I didn't have to take Bill's junk anymore. I'd stuck it to him good. I would later learn that life has a way of showing us how other people feel when we hurt them.

In the next chapter, we'll explore the power of expectation. Difficult circumstances are hard enough to deal with, but even more so when we assume a rosy result, and get an even thornier situation instead.

UNPACKING YOUR SHOEBOX

The Shoebox Sherpa's Points to Ponder

- When we think we're keeping secrets, we are actually imprisoned by them. You can only experience freedom when secrets are revealed.

- Unresolved fears often come out as anger. When you feel mad, ask yourself if you are really afraid of something.

- Just because we tell ourselves we are justified does not mean we truly are. Do not allow yourself to rationalize what you know is wrong.

- The patterns of self-destruction are typically grounded in childhood. Make a timeline of your life, and search for pinnacle moments that may have convinced you that you don't deserve good things.

1. Have any of your secrets ever caused an angry response—in yourself or others? Was fear a factor?

   _____

   _____

   _____

   _____

2. Can you think of a time when a past wound caused you to do something you regretted or that hurt other people? ___

   _____

   _____

   _____

   _____

CHAPTER SIX

SHATTERED SHOES

Expectations, assumptions, suppositions—this is the stuff of confusion and conflict—the kind that kicks you in the gut and keeps you down for a while.

I had filed for divorce, located a job, and was beginning to settle into my new apartment located at the opposite end of town. My landlord listened to me compassionately as I spun my tale of woe. He let me move in with no security deposit, and even turned the utilities on with only a promise to pay my monthly rent on time. I felt liberated.

My apartment was actually an old house that had been remodeled into three apartments, mine was the largest one. The downstairs kitchen had an open living room, nice-sized laundry room, and a half-bath, plus beautiful bay windows to let the morning sunlight in. The upstairs housed two bedrooms and a full bath, with another smaller room that I used as a playroom for Michele. My favorite part was the fireplace in the living room; it was just like the one we'd had in Indiana growing up. I could not wait for the seasons to change so I could start my first flames.

My mother mailed me a housewarming box with a lovely pair of bright yellow kitchen curtains and a book entitled, *The Power of Positive Thinking*[3]. The enclosed letter expressed her concern for Michele and me. I groaned when I read, *Will you please reconsider moving to Indianapolis?*

---

3 https://www.amazon.com/Power-Positive-Thinking-Norman-Vincent/dp/9388118561/

I put the letter up and got to work. I hung the curtains and tossed the book into a pile of other self-help books she'd sent me. I knew she meant well, intending to encourage me and set me on a better path. But I was focused on other things.

Settling In

Roger helped me move. Borrowing a truck from a friend of his, he showed up with more manpower, and as a team, we emptied the small house I had shared with Bill. I left nothing but the appliances and the bedroom suite.

Neither Bill nor I had any sadness or anger about the ending of our marriage. In fact, after the initial shockwave, Bill finally confessed that he, too, had been having an affair. Within a few weeks, he had moved his girlfriend in to his place.

Bill and I continued our shared custody arrangement of Michele, enacted when we separated. He picked her up from the sitter's every Thursday at 5:15 p.m. and drove to the country. On Sundays, he brought her back to me by 6:00 p.m.

I was enjoying the best of all my worlds.

Roger stopped by every evening after he got off work. He showered at my house instead of going to his place first, and had dinner with Michele and me. Sometimes we went out, but mostly, we ate in.

I loved doing the dishes and looking out my kitchen window to see Roger pushing my daughter on the swing or playing tag. Michele would squeal with delight as he chased her around the yard. After we put her to bed, we were finally alone for a few hours of our own play. No matter how wonderful our time together on Monday through Wednesday, Roger always left for home before midnight. His nightly absence only added anticipation and built my excitement. I couldn't remember feeling happier. There was only one problem. My sister.

When Judy found out about Roger and me, she thundered her disapproval. "Are you out of your mind?"

The strength of her reaction made no sense to me. "Why can't you be happy for us?"

"Because I know exactly how this is going to end. You are going to get hurt, just like all the other women he's wooed. It will never work. Do you honestly think he is going to marry you? Are you so naïve to think you are the only one he's seeing? He's a player, Marcie. He has nothing to offer you."

Marry me? I hadn't even considered that. We never discussed living together, let alone marriage. What was she talking about? Yes, I was crazy about him. Yes, I wanted to be with him. But marriage? I had no expectations of a proposal.

"Jute, please, just be happy for me. I don't know where this is going, but for right now, I feel truly wanted."

Judy wouldn't accept him. The protectiveness my older sister had for me started when I was a small child and had never waned. Even when I didn't or couldn't see trouble, she sniffed it out on my behalf and went into guardian mode. Years later, we laughed about it and called it Sister Radar—but early in the summer of 1977, neither of us were laughing. I left her house crying, her last words still ringing in my ears.

"I love you Marcie, and my home is always open to you," she said with a tinge of sadness to her tone. "And I will be here for you when the time comes to pick up the pieces. You're going to need me. But don't bring him around. He won't be welcome."

How I prayed she would be wrong. It would be decades before I fully understood the depth of Judy's love and the reason for her agony on my behalf. She was hiding her own dark secrets behind a mask of sisterly ferocity. But at this time, I still hadn't found her box.

Mission on My Own

As the seasons changed, so did my relationship with Roger. After six months, I could not imagine my daily life without him in it. I envisioned a future for us with my daughter, and soon forgot my sister's warning.

The excitement of the Christmas holidays had already begun at the Adamstown Rod and Gun Club—a local social gathering place that also hosted community events. Roger and I, along with two other couples, spent an early Saturday morning decorating the tree and hanging tinsel throughout the building. We were already making plans for the popular New Year's Eve dance.

When I arrived home later in the day, I surveyed my closet for an outfit to wear to the dance. After several minutes it became obvious I needed to go shopping.

Judy has such great taste—she'll help me pick out the right dress. As soon as that thought hit my mind, my heart sank. She still had not warmed up to Roger. If I wanted to see or call her, I had to do it without him around. And I doubted she'd want anything to do with me making myself look sexy for a night out with the man of my youthful dreams. I'd have to do this solo.

Roger agreed to keep Michele for me one evening so I could drive to the Lancaster Mall in search of my holiday dress. Sadness accompanied me.

I missed Judy and really wanted her with me today. She would know just what kind of dress I should buy. I imagined my sister pulling me in and out of stores and holding dresses up under my chin, like she did when I was little. Her face always told me which ones were her favorites, but the perfect outfit made her eyes sparkle. I could hear her say in a half shout, half whisper, "That's the one, Mace, that's the one."

A sales clerk interrupted my reflections.

"How can I help you?"

After trying several dresses on, I chose an onyx mini with little black straps to match. I recalled how both my mother and sister had the standard "little black dress" for their special occasions. I'd heard Judy say you could never go wrong when you wore black. She said it always stayed fashionable and made an especially great contrast with blonde hair—the shade of my strands.

The sales clerk helped me find a matching handbag and a pair of rhinestone earrings to add polished touches. After putting everything on, I surveyed myself in the full-length mirror. I couldn't believe it was me.

The dress was deceptive from the front with its simple, but classic look. The real surprise presented in the back. There wasn't one—or much of one. Small, colored jewels covered what sparse material there was. It was perfect. I felt pleased with myself, having accomplished a mission on my own.

I packed up my car and headed home, anxious to show Roger. I was totally unprepared for what I found.

Walking through the front door of my apartment, I immediately breathed in the familiar scent of pine. It was one of my favorite nostalgic fragrances. I traced the smell to my living room, where a fully decorated Christmas tree stood. Nearby, a wreath and three red stockings hung above the crackling logs in my fireplace. I was speechless.

Michele clapped her little hands in excitement. "Oh, Mommy, isn't it purdy? We did it. Me and Woger, we did it."

And then I was enfolded in a double embrace from my two favorite people.

Roger said, "Did we surprise you?"

Surprised wasn't the word. I was overcome. "Yes! Thank you. I can't believe you did all this."

Michele started gushing, telling me about their escapades as she and Roger got the tree in the house. She described Roger slipping in the snow and falling, making "yummy hot chocolate," and his riotous hunt for the Christmas decorations. She smiled and laughed through the whole thing.

I smiled back and thought, *Kid, you're making my soul melt. Could anything be more perfect?*

Caught up in my daughter's excitement, I forgot all about the dress, until Roger let me know he hadn't. "Show me what you bought."

I started to pull my dress out of its shopping bag.

"Don't show it to me that way," he said. "Go put it on. I want to see you in it."

Ten minutes later, I made my way down the steps into my beautifully decorated living room. As I surveyed Roger and Michele's faces, I felt like a queen. I pretended to be on a catwalk and sashayed over to the fireplace, then spun around. Roger nodded an approval. But he wasn't quite satisfied yet.

"Go upstairs and put on a pair of your black fishnet stockings," he insisted.

"All right," I said. Obediently, I went upstairs, happy to make myself even more beautiful for him.

When I came down the second time, the glisten in Roger's eyes and his wolf whistle set electricity off in my limbs. I made my catwalk moves by the fireplace a second time.

"Beautiful," he said softly. "So beautiful."

It was the second time I'd heard those words in that tone. The octave of his voice had changed, as if it held a hidden meaning that only he understood.

That evening, however, I took Roger's response as an honest compliment and nothing more. I did not know about the shame or secrets he kept hidden behind those amazing eyes of his. Roger's shoebox was purely emotional. I did not notice his brokenness reflected throughout our relationship, rearing its ugly head subtly, begging to be dealt with.

Picture Perfect

I ran into Roger's open arms and kissed him. "It is beautiful isn't it?" I said softly. "I'm so excited, I can't wait for New Year's Eve." Then I reached down and picked up my toddler, squeezing her tightly. I planted a light kiss on her forehead. "I love you honey, thank you for my surprise."

She grinned back at me, "I love you too, Mommy. Is Santa coming tonight?"

"Soon, sweetie, soon," I said as I began to slow dance with her in my arms. Roger watched us both with a pensive smile on his lips.

Christmas Eve, my living room sparkled, displaying all the familiar traditions from holidays past. It took me back to the smell of pine and popcorn, as Daddy shook the wire mesh box by its long, metal handle over the open fire, until the last kernel snapped. We were always home on Christmas Eve, together as a family. It was the one time things were good during my childhood.

This year, my house mimicked what I saw in my mind. Everything appeared picture perfect—except for one thing.

Michele was at the farm with Bill. Roger was with his family. Judy was still angry. I sat alone on the floor near the tree, eating a peanut butter and jelly sandwich off of a plain, white paper towel while I watched *The Jeffersons* on TV. Merry Christmas to me.

An Unaffordable Cost

By New Year's Eve, I'd stuffed my depressive thoughts and replaced them with exciting plans. I had my first adult dance to look forward to, along with my first adult dress, and would share them both with the man I wanted to be with.

We arrived at the club early. Roger did his usual—charming friends and acquaintances while he worked the room. I stood demurely by his side, feeling like the king's queen, as I waited for him to introduce me to those I didn't know. Being with Roger made me feel wanted, accepted, and important—I was not accustomed to this kind of fairytale attention. I still had trouble believing he was mine.

When the music started, Roger grabbed my hand, pulled me close, and danced me effortlessly around the floor. I threw my head back and laughed freely. The whole evening, we danced until I was breathless. I never wanted the music to end.

Near midnight, a song gave up its final chord and Floyd Kramer began to play "The Last Date." There was a smoky sexiness to the slow piano beat, unhindered by vocal distraction. The way Roger gripped me when he pulled me even tighter told me to prepare myself. But I still wasn't ready when he brushed my ear with his mouth and said, "I love you, you know."

If I questioned his power over me before, there was no denying it now. Every part of me belonged to him, body, mind, and spirit. I just didn't realize there was a cost—and it was one I really couldn't afford.

A few months later, on an ordinary weekday morning in April, I prepared my omelet before heading to work. I often sautéed green peppers on the stove, but this time, they started my gag reflex. I dashed to the bathroom. After wiping my mouth with a wet cloth, I thought. *Why am I feeling sick? Surely, it's not the peppers—I always eat them in my eggs.*

I took a mental inventory of everything I had ingested the day before. Nothing unusual came to mind.

This new routine repeated itself the next morning, and the one after, and the one after that. Several days later, with no relief, I decided I'd better see the doctor a friend recommended.

Dr. Stanley confirmed what I suspected. I was pregnant.

The Perfect Mood

I couldn't wait to tell Roger. Granted, this was not a planned pregnancy, but Roger loved children, was good with Michele, and he loved me. The four of us would become my ideal family. Michele would make a wonderful big sister, and Judy would finally accept Roger. Daddy might even let me come home. My dreams were finally coming true.

I wanted to create the perfect mood. Michele was with her dad, so I could go all out.

I made Roger's favorite meal—Swiss steak roasted in the oven for hours. By the time he walked through my front door, the savory, mouthwatering aroma had permeated the entire house.

Gently placing a kiss at the nape of my neck, he whispered, "Headed to the shower, wanna join me?"

I giggled, tempted by his offer, and said, "There's plenty of time for that later." I needed to finish the preparations for our perfect night.

We finished our delicious meal, including the creamy whipped potatoes and Parmesan buttered green beans that enhanced the steak. I left all the dishes on the table and invited Roger to join me in the living room.

He sat next to me on my brown plaid couch and I took his hands in mine. We faced each other. My heart fluttered. I moved my hands and placed them on his knees. In a single, flawless moment, I leaned in and very softly uttered the words, "I'm pregnant," then waited for him to share in my joy.

A blank stare came first.

Where's his smile?

Roger furrowed his brow and cocked his head to the side, before he unleashed his disappointment. "I'm not ready to be a father, Marcie. What were you thinking? You know I'm not the marrying kind. How could you let this happen?" His words delivered their intended blow.

Stunned and in shock, I couldn't form a verbal response. Mentally, I had plenty to say. *How are you not happy about this? I didn't plan it, but this is good news. Doctors told me I'd never be able to have kids again, so this is a miracle. A beautiful miracle between two people who love each other. How can you not understand?* I withdrew my hands from his knees and sat back on the sofa.

Roger kept ranting.

Don't You Dare Cry

No matter how loud he got or how awful the things he said, I resolved to hold my tears back. *Don't you dare cry,* I told myself. I refused to make eye contact and averted my eyes. While Roger raged, I distracted myself by picking at my fresh manicure—chipping away vivid fuchsia nail polish.

Infuriated and seeing he was getting no response, Roger stood. I heard his deliberate, heavy footsteps as he made his way briskly up the stairs. *Slam!* I heard the bedroom door thud as the ceiling above me shook from the force.

No longer able to restrain my shock and sadness, I surrendered. My tears quickly turned to sobs. With Roger in my bedroom, I stayed on the couch and cried myself to sleep.

The next morning, after a fitful night's sleep, I awoke in the fog of an emotional hangover. Last night's traumatic scene pushed its way to the forefront of my mind. Before I even pried my puffy, swollen eyelids open, I knew what waited for me.

Dirty dishes sat on the kitchen table and cold food remained in serving dishes. *My perfect meal. What a catastrophe.*

I mustered the will to open my eyes. Seeing it made my brain connect with the sensation of something covering me from shoulders to toes. Sometime during the night or maybe in the early morning hours, Roger had draped my favorite wedding ring quilt over my body. *Maybe he's changing his mind.* The tender gesture stirred renewed hope.

Making Up

I ignored the dinner mess and pushed myself through my morning ritual. I had to get ready for work. Though Roger had slipped out earlier, I assumed the quilt meant a different kind of conversation that night. I thought about it all day.

After work, I was anxious to get home and see Roger. I imagined us talking things through, making up, and then making up some more—upstairs. But I couldn't shake my underlying feeling of dread. *How did last night even happen?*

Hoping to beat Roger and freshen up before he arrived, I turned the knob to my front door and burst in. Then I froze.

The first thing I spied was Roger's set of keys to my house placed on top of a stereo speaker. I ran to the bathroom and frantically opened the closet—his toiletries were missing. I didn't need to guess what this meant. I made the short walk into the living room and dropped into my chair with a humph. I started to hang my head in my hands when I noticed a white envelope, placed on top of my stereo.

I walked over and picked it up. The outside was blank—just like my soul. I opened the letter and read the short lines.

Don't come looking for me. I can never be the man you want. I'm a loser. Do yourself a favor and forget all about me.

The envelope contained something more—cash. Based on the amount, I assumed this money implied his wish for me to have an abortion. My sister's words of warning pounded in my ears. I dropped the letter in disbelief. How could this be happening?

When we want and expect a particular outcome, but life throws us a version we neither anticipated nor desired, it can throw us into an emotional tailspin. We may say or do things unusual to our nature. Has this ever happened to you?

Grief takes the messy and turns it into complete chaos. Next, I'll give you an insider's glimpse into my own everyday cray-cray, as I tried to make sense of Roger's abandonment. Sometimes, we simply don't care what we look like.

UNPACKING YOUR SHOEBOX

The Shoebox Sherpa's Points to Ponder

- When your emotions are swirling, ask yourself what you can validate with evidence in order to protect yourself from conjecture that leads to greater conflict.

- To prevent misunderstandings and misinterpretations, ask clarifying questions. "If I heard you correctly, you said . . ." "When you said _____, did you mean _____?"

- If you want to lift your spirits, dedicate yourself to reading at least one book on positivity per month—especially if your world has come crashing down.

- As much as possible, get adequate rest when an emotional event occurs. The less sleep we get, the less we are able to handle stressful situations well.

1. Have you ever missed subtle or not-so-subtle signs pointing to impending danger? What was the outcome?

   _____

   _____

   _____

   _____

2. When life and people disappoint you, how do you typically respond? Is your way healthy? If not, what might you begin doing differently to help you cope?

   _____

   _____

   _____

   _____

CHAPTER SEVEN

EVERYDAY CRAY-CRAY

H ave you ever been forced to deal with someone else's decision that was made in polar opposition to your own desires? How did you react? In hindsight, are there things you wish you would have done differently?

When I've discussed this topic with others, most people I've talked with have at least one story of their own to tell. In many private and confidential conversations, I've received confirmation that most of us handle disappointment poorly, at least initially. Under the right (or wrong) conditions, we can all go a little everyday cray-cray. Some of us just take it to a higher level.

I disregarded Roger's words not to come looking for him. How dare he tell me I couldn't? I was carrying his child, after all. Whether he intended to help me parent or not, he still had a responsibility to us. Or so I thought.

Everyone soon knew I was pregnant with Roger's baby, from our friends and family to the neighbors. My "situation" provided a great topic of conversation at the VFW Post and Bowman's Hat Factory, where many of the Adamstown residents were employed. I ignored their looks and snide, under-the-breath comments. I didn't find it hard to disregard the gossip, but after Roger's rejection, one other person's abandonment completely broke my heart.

I had contemplated returning to Southern Indiana until Daddy laid down the law to me via Marge, my step-mother. "I'm sorry, honey," she said. "Your daddy won't budge. He told me to tell you, 'Don't come home.'"

I was devastated by the sense of aloneness I felt. After a few days of grieving the loss of emotional support from the two men I loved most, I took a deep breath and pulled my big girl pants on. In my mind, Daddy's directive left me no recourse but to make the best of things where I was at. That included keeping an eye on the father of my baby.

On the Hunt

I started out just driving around town, looking for any signs of Roger's silver Oldsmobile. *Perhaps if he just sees my swollen belly, he will change his mind,* I thought. Surely, after all the love and passion we shared, he had to be thinking of us. Right? *He will come around,* I told myself. *He just needs time.*

One Saturday morning, I walked into the post office and overheard a brunette talking about her date the previous evening. The moment she said Roger's name, we locked eyes. She froze when I stepped up to gather my mail.

I knew who she was, Roger had told me all about this particular brunette and his previous entanglement with her when we were dating. Apparently, she also recognized me. I fought the urge to pounce on her, and instead, proudly displayed my protruding belly. I wanted to get under her skin. I couldn't tell how well it worked, but I knew she'd sure gotten under mine. And she would not be the only one.

In the small town of Adamstown, Roger was everywhere. Every day, I drove obsessively around town, on the hunt to find him, driving myself cray-cray at the same time.

By the time October came around, I'd seen Dr Stanley for quite a while. With each office visit, he continually talked to me about adoption, and increased the pressure for me to surrender my child. However, I was still not ready to even think about making that kind of decision. *Roger will come through,* I told myself.

One day, Dr. Stanley mentioned the issue of the future birth certificate. This gave me the perfect excuse to talk to Roger, we needed to resolve this before our baby's birth. I spotted his car at the Adamstown Rod and Gun Club, so I parked and walked in. He was sitting at the bar with a blonde next to him, her possessive hand on his knee. The boiling in my veins gave me just the courage I needed.

Good Signs

Roger hadn't seen me yet, so I caught him off-guard when I marched into their space, ignoring the bleach-blonde vixen. "We need to talk," I said.

He nodded silently, then rose from the bar stool.

I shot the blonde a dirty look before proudly walking outside with Roger. At this point, I was happy with any small victory over the women I saw as getting between me and the man I loved. I'd certainly seen plenty of them as I'd compulsively chased him around town over the past few months.

As we stood outside the bar, Roger mostly listened, though he struggled to make eye contact. He played with the gravel covering the parking lot, pushing it around with his toes.

After making some brief and uneasy small talk, I got to the point. I spewed, "Dr. Stanley keeps talking to me about adoption."

Roger instantly stopped scuffing the ground with his shoe, but he still spoke without looking at me. "Might be a good idea. Worth considering, anyway. Maybe you should give it some thought."

I dismissed his comment. "I have to decide what to do about the birth certificate. What am I supposed to put under the father's name?"

Roger finally looked up. "Do whatever you want. Makes no difference to me. I'm sorry you're having to deal with all this."

Exasperated, I spun around and walked away.

Driving home, I replayed Roger's few words. The more I thought about it, the more I actually saw hope in how he'd responded. He made no promises, but he didn't insist I put the baby up for adoption either. And he did say he was sorry.

At the time, I thought this hopeful sign made it clear we weren't done. There was still time for Roger to step up and rescue us. I missed the part where he clearly took himself out of the equation.

Once I'd announced my pregnancy, Roger's visits to the Turkey Hill store where I was an assistant manager had stopped abruptly. However, six weeks before my due date, he began to show up again. I took it as a good sign. I could tell he was thinking about me and our baby.

Almost every day I worked, Roger stopped by. He'd pick up the newspaper and read the sports page at the counter. Then he'd nonchalantly ask after my health, as if he were discussing the weather. "How ya feelin'?"

I played along, believing a calm demeanor would draw him back. "Fine," I'd say." We played our little "casual conversation" game between customers.

As a part of this new routine, before leaving, Roger would lean in over the counter and place a tender kiss on my forehead, leaving me with a false hope that we weren't over.

The Inevitable

On a Saturday night in early October, I huddled in my house while the cold, fall rain fell on my roof. I'd just settled into my comfortable green robe and made a cup of hot tea, ready to watch television before bed. A loud knock on the front door of my house made me grumble.

I pulled the curtain back and saw Roger's Oldsmobile out front. He hadn't been to my house since he left the note for me the night after I told him I was pregnant. My pulse accelerated.

I got up and opened the door. Roger's hair was saturated, and as he entered, he dripped on my foyer rug. I noticed he held a small bag in his hands.

"I brought you some chili from the club," he said, as if we were still comfortably a couple and nothing had changed over the past few months. "Corky was cooking today. He asked about you."

I opened the paper sack and let the spicy delicious aroma fill my nostrils. The bag also contained several packets of crackers. Corky's nickname for me was "Crackers" and he always gave me extra, as our little secret.

I pulled a plastic spoon and some bar napkins out of the bag. When I reached back in, I discovered a hand-scrawled note. It said, "We miss you, Crackers. Love, Corky."

I smiled at the kind gesture. For the last year, I'd filled the role of club secretary. I enjoyed using my talents to serve the organization and its members, and I missed it. Corky was president and had promised I could have the secretary's position back when I was ready. I loved taking the minutes in shorthand and transcribing them for the book of records. The job made me proud of the skills I had acquired while in high school, and especially grateful for my stepmother, Marge, who urged me to master this complicated task.

"Tell Corky thank you for me. Would you like to come in?" I said, as if Roger was a mere friend or acquaintance dropping by.

Roger nodded and followed me to the couch. He removed his jacket and sat beside me.

I took a sip of my tea and waited for him to speak. I could smell alcohol on his breath.

After a few minutes of awkward silence, I got up and left the room. He didn't question me. When I returned, I brought him a towel and instinctively began to blot his wet hair.

Roger reached out for my hand and pulled me closer. In one deft motion, he gently untied my robe and exposed my swollen body. With hands on both sides of our child, he gently lowered his head and placed his face against the skin on my belly. Wordlessly, he just lay there, holding me and our child. I dared not move.

Moments later, I heard a familiar sound. Roger's breathing had changed, signaling sleep. For a moment, the warmth of his body and soft, rhythmic snores made me feel secure. I'd dreamed of having him back. I decided to let him spend the night.

Afraid to disturb the father of my child, I carefully adjusted my couch pillow to allow me some rest. I turned my face so I could muffle the sound of my tears, then prayed the morning sun would never come up. And yet, I knew.

This would be the last night I would get to lay in Roger's arms. After months of obsessively clinging to hope and chasing Roger around town, I knew I had to get a grip on myself and the reality of my situation. As much as I didn't want to do it, the first thing in the morning, I had a phone call to make. I'd made my decision.

Confusion and a few moments of cray-cray are part of grieving any situation, whether it's due to the physical death of a loved one, or the emotional death of something we hoped not to lose. When you better understand the shoebox effect, you learn to expect it and to give yourself a dose of grace. It's okay to not be okay with a major loss.

Accepting the inevitable is actually a part of mourning, and signals you are on your way to healing. The sting of pain will still exist, but so will a few sparks of inner strength, even if they don't seem to last very long. All of this is normal when you are dealing with an abnormal circumstance. Grief is messy, after all.

After some time of feeling scared, lonely, and getting tired of the discomfort, we begin to seek hope, encouragement, and support. Occasionally, it comes in surprising packages—and they aren't always bold or big. A whisper will do. Next, I'll share how a tiny inspiration helped me in a massive way.

UNPACKING YOUR SHOEBOX

1. When have you obsessed over a problem, chasing it around and around in your head? How did it help? How did it drive you even crazier? _____

   _____

   _____

   _____

   _____

2. Have you ever allowed other people's opinions, thoughts, and gossip to shape your decisions? How do you differentiate between wise counsel and foolish advice? _____

   _____

   _____

   _____

   _____

The Shoebox Sherpa's Points to Ponder

- Remember, you cannot control anyone else, you can hope to influence, but their decisions are their own. Instead of trying to change another person, work on changing you.

- Give yourself permission to feel your grief when faced with a loss of any kind. Yes, emotions get messy, but when you process them instead of stuffing, you will heal faster.

- Pay attention to what you're telling yourself. Is it healthy? If not, work hard to change that inner dialogue.

- Give yourself grace when you feel temporarily cray-cray, then decide to act with the dignity you deserve.

.

CHAPTER EIGHT

JIMINY CRICKET MOMENTS

Any event that leads us toward the shoebox effect can sap us of our inner strength. The question becomes, will we allow this to steal our hope permanently, or will we feel what we need to feel, and then take action to overcome?

Tangible symbols make great healthy triggers when we need a boost of motivation and inspiration. I found mine back when I was a child. Still today, I feel supported and encouraged from something you might find surprising. A quiet, affirming whisper can shout positivity into your soul.

I had gambled and lost. A sick feeling of helplessness and panic set in, as soon as I realized Roger was going to leave me when I needed him the most. Last night's visit was nothing more than his weak attempt at removing the guilt he felt. He didn't come back to stay—he showed up to say good-bye to me and our baby.

In the morning, it became apparent he agreed with Dr. Stanley. Adoption was the only answer. The bile rose up in my throat just thinking about why this was an especially hard hit for me. I'd been abandoned before.

I recognized the pain when Roger walked out of my life without a backward glance, yet I couldn't fully process the fact that it was happening again. I was taken back to my five-year-old self and a 1960 event embedded in my soul. Mommy had told me it was going to be our special day—but she didn't say she'd be gone the next.

A Magical Day

Daddy had already left for work by the time I got up that morning. Sissy and my brother, Butchie, were both in school. Mommy said it was our special secret and not to tell anyone. I inhaled the scent of her perfume and watched as her bright, violet-blue eyes danced with excitement about our big adventure.

She brushed my long, blonde hair and slipped a tiny gold bracelet with a pretty purple stone on my wrist. I couldn't say the long name of the jewel, but it was obvious Mommy treasured it, just like she treasured me. It was my first introduction to an Amethyst—the color representing my birthday month—February.

After we'd gotten all dressed up, Mommy and I walked over to the hall mirror and surveyed our appearances. I took in a tiny breath and smiled. I thought we looked like something from one of my fairy-tale books.

My silky, black and white, hound's tooth dress felt as soft as velvet and made me feel like a big girl. A big girl like my Sissy.

At five, I called my sister, Judy, Sissy, or by our family nickname, Jute. Older by eight years, my five-year-old self watched Sissy's every move and mimicked what I could.

A member of Job's Daughters, a Masonic-affiliated youth organization for young girls, Judy and my female cousins would prance around in their lacy white formals like they were Disney princesses preparing for big events. If I cried to join them, Sissy would soothe me and tell her I was *her* princess. That always made me feel better.

On this day, however, I really was a princess. Mommy said so.

I followed Mommy's instructions and watched out our big picture window for Velma Hanson's car. I kneeled on the couch and rested my head on my crossed arms, while I waited for Velma to come pick us up. I couldn't wait to start the beautiful day Mommy had described.

Velma and my mom were not only former neighbors, but they were also close friends. It ran in the family. Daddy was friends with Velma's husband, and Velma's daughter, Fran, and I were born just one month apart. She was my best friend. There was no one I'd rather share a secret escapade with than Fran.

When I finally saw Velma's car pull into our driveway I squealed. "Mommy, Mommy. They're here."

"Good girl, Marcie. Now, let's go have some fun," Mommy said.

As we made our way across the Kennedy Bridge into Louisville, Kentucky, Mommy told us what we were going to do. "First, you're going to get your pictures taken at a professional photography studio. Then, we'll eat lunch by the river at the King Fish. And if you girls are especially good, we're going to take you to be on the T-Bar-V show." (It was a popular children's morning show at the time.)

Fran and I hugged each other tightly, then bounced up and down on the sedan's wide, leather seat. Every few minutes, one of us asked, "Are we there, yet?"

Mommy answered "no," patiently every time, until finally, she said, "Yes."

Fran and I squealed again.

The entire day with Mommy was magical. Back then, we never went out to eat and hardly ever crossed the bridge from Southern Indiana into Louisville. Mommy and Velma bought Fran and I some new clothes, and my best friend and I got to be on our favorite show. Our last stop, however, confused me.

Daddy's sister, Aunt Helen, always trimmed our hair. So, it didn't make sense that Mommy took me to a beauty salon.

I climbed up into the black, swivel chair, unsure of what to expect. In minutes, it was over. When my hands touched the back of my head, I could feel my bare neck. As I felt around more, seeking my familiar ponytail, I was shocked to find nothing. My blonde, Rapunzel locks were gone.

Strangely Quiet

The next morning, I awoke to shouting. Nothing unusual, Mommy and Daddy were always yelling. I often felt afraid as their voices raised and their tones flattened. But something about this sounded different—it scared me more than normal. I reached out for Sissy, but she wasn't in our bed.

I pulled the covers over my head and curled up against the wall, clutching my teddy bear. My chin quivered as I wondered if I'd be safer staying hidden.

Daddy screeched obscenities at Mommy. They sounded like dark, ominous words, though I had no idea what they meant. I just knew they were bad. I could hear Sissy crying and telling him to stop. I clung to my teddy's neck and closed my eyes as tight as possible, hoping I could make myself disappear. Then I heard a loud smack and thump.

I cautiously got out of bed and tip-toed toward the commotion. As I neared the kitchen, the scent of spices filled the air. When I got to the doorway leading into the kitchen, I stopped walking.

My beautiful Mommy lay on the kitchen floor surrounded by broken spice jars and a splintered rack. She was limp, like my favorite rag doll.

Daddy stood over Mommy, but he must have heard me. When he turned in my direction, his foot tapped the edge of a nearly intact bottle, and it began to roll slowly on the spotted linoleum floor, resting near Daddy's breakfast chair. I wondered why he wasn't sitting at the table, eating his eggs and bacon like he did most mornings.

As I surveyed everyone and the condition of our kitchen in the now hushed room, I also wondered if I had somehow caused this. *What did I do?* My feet suddenly warmed. I looked down to see a puddle of yellow liquid forming below me. I had wet myself.

Suddenly, Mommy, looking at my feet—began to cry.

Sissy ushered me back to our room, cleaned me up, and kept me occupied the rest of the day.

The next morning, I woke up to find my sister gone again. I didn't like the cold her absence left in the bed. The smell of bacon was also missing. The house sounded strangely quiet.

When I entered the living room, Daddy was slumped over on the couch. I could see that his olive skin was wet with tears. Daddy never cried. Sissy sat stoically in the easy chair.

"Where's Mommy?" I said. "I'm hungry."

My sister said nothing, but immediately ran from the room in tears.

Daddy stated flatly, "Your mother's gone and she's not coming back."

Instinctively, I reached up for a piece of my shoulder-length, blonde hair. I had a habit of twisting it between my fingers when I felt nervous or scared. But like my Mommy, after our big adventure, those long locks were absent.

Story About a Boy

I was taken to my Aunt Helen's the same day. In her gentle, motherly way, she tried to explain to me that though my Mommy was gone, I would see her sometime in the future. What does a five-year-old know about the future?

"You mean today?" I asked innocently. "I want my Mommy."

Aunt Helen said, "Do you want a treat?"

I nodded yes, as curiosity temporarily distracted me from my fears and confusion.

Aunt Helen took me by the hand and walked me to her bedroom closet. She dug around for a few minutes.

While she bustled, I stared at the yellow, Whitman's Chocolate box, high on the shelf above Aunt Helen's head.

"Do you want one?" she said without turning around.

"Uh, huh," I said. But how did she know what I was looking at?

Aunt Helen straightened her back and reached for the Whitman's box. She had always amazed me with her ability to see the unseen. She always knew what was in each piece of candy before you pulled it apart or bit into it. These intriguing skills made me believe her when she said, "I have eyes in the back of my head." Of course, she could simply see out of her peripheral vision and read the Whitman's chocolate guide, printed on the box.

"Climb up here on the bed," Aunt Helen said as she made her way across the room. She patted a spot next to her. "But eat your chocolate first, so you don't get any on my quilt."

I popped the rest of the candy in my mouth and let the swirl of peanut butter and chocolate melt over my tongue.

"Let me see your hands," Aunt Helen said. After a quick inspection, she muttered, "Just a little." Then she leaned toward her night stand and pulled a tissue from the box on top, spit on it, and gently pulled my little hands into her lap. She rubbed the small smudge of chocolate off. "All better. Now, upsy-daisy."

After I carefully crawled up, I scooted in close. Aunt Helen wore Heaven Scent perfume, and I thought she smelled like an angel. I didn't notice the bag until I settled in beside her.

"I'm going to read you a story about a boy. I think it will help you when you feel sad. It's okay, you know. You're going to stay with me for a while, and I expect you'll feel sad at first. I understand that."

"But why can't I go home with Daddy and Mommy?" My chin began to quiver.

"Things are going to change, Marcie. I wish the situation was different, but it's not. Your Mommy's going away."

I started to cry.

Aunt Helen put her arm around me and cooed. "There, there. I know."

Choking on my words as I spoke, I said, "I think I made Mommy go away."

Concern tinged Aunt Helen's voice. "Why would you say that, honey?"

"Because when Daddy and Mommy were fighting, I got scared and closed my eyes real tight to make the hurt go away. I wanted to disappear. Maybe Mommy went away because I disappeared."

Aunt Helen chuckled softly. "Remember the story about the little boy I told you about? He was sad, too. But a friend helped him feel better, and he taught him what to do when the boy felt bad." She pulled a colorful book onto her lap. "I'm going to read you a story called Pinocchio."

As Aunt Helen read, the Jiminy Cricket character interested me even more so than the puppet who became a boy. Jiminy was small like me, but we differed because he seemed to always know what to do. At the end of the story, I felt so happy for Pinocchio, and I wished I had a Jiminy Cricket to help me. Aunt Helen once again read my mind.

A Sense of Security

She laid the book down and picked up the bag beside her. She reached her hand inside and pulled out a Jiminy Cricket mask. She held it toward me and said, "When you put this mask on, you can be strong and feel all the sadness you need to feel, instead of making yourself disappear. And when your mommy comes back to visit you—and she will—you can put this mask on, and she will always be able to see you. Okay?"

Little, five-year-old Marcie felt relieved, knowing she wouldn't disappear again, and that Mommy wouldn't cry. Marcie could always be seen because of the mask.

Throughout my childhood, Aunt Helen read Pinocchio to me, over and over. Later, she got me a Jiminy Cricket stuffed animal. He became my childhood friend and keeper of my secrets. Though I threw the tattered and torn mask away when I was thirteen, I kept my precious Jiminy Cricket stuffed animal. I no longer needed a mask, but I did need a sense of security to lean on—even into adulthood. I still have him today.

As an adult, when I feel scared, sad, or confused, I have what I and my family call a Jiminy Cricket moment, where I go off to myself, and take all of my concerns to my trusted, imaginary friend. It may seem silly to some people, but having a tangible symbol to confide in helps me feel what I need to feel, instead of burying my emotions. It helps me process the truth in a healthy way.

I needed Jiminy when Roger and I attempted a reconciliation. However, the situation did not end as I planned. Roger blindsided me once again—causing me to turn back to Jiminy for inner strength. I'm not sure I would have survived, if it hadn't been for the coping mechanism of that tattered, old cricket. He listened when I had no one else. But instead of continuing to use Jiminy to process my feelings, I eventually shelved him and picked something else up in his place. It was not the better choice.

I hid my emotions and my truth in the shoebox effect once more. By doing so, it turned me into someone else. I came to call her the consummate actress.

UNPACKING YOUR SHOEBOX

1. Do you have a tangible symbol that provides you with inner strength and hope? _____

_____

_____

_____

_____

2. How do you process your emotions when a challenge, difficulty, or crisis hits? Is stuffing or facing your feelings your go-to?

_____

_____

_____

_____

_____

The Shoebox Sherpa's Points to Ponder

• Think back through your life. Has a particular sign or symbol strengthened you or increased your peace? If so, get some kind of tangible memento that you can easily turn to when facing a difficult moment or season. Having something to hold on to eases the mind and quiets the spirit.

• If you struggle with abandonment or rejection issues from the past and haven't allowed yourself to face the pain or mourn your loss, study the known stages of grief or read books on the subject, and give yourself permission to cleanse your soul now.

• Expressing gratitude is a powerful way to move through and overcome painful emotions. Each day, choose one person, place, or thing you are thankful for, and focus on it, versus letting past hurts hold you in an emotional prison.

• Become the emotional parent your inner child needs. It's okay to offer yourself support, encouragement, and love.

CHAPTER NINE

SELECTING THE SHOEBOX

We all know there are consequences connected to choices, but for some reason, we don't always expect them in our own circumstances—or at least not in the way they present. Have you ever been blindsided by a cause and effect?

I don't claim to understand why many of us seem determined to learn lessons by taking the most difficult route possible. In my case, I've circled over the all-too-familiar-terrain repeatedly.

Several weeks before my due date, Jute called. "I'd like you to consider bringing Michele and staying with me, at least until after the baby comes. I hate thinking of you being alone. I'll even go to your doctor's appointments with you, if you'd like."

Her concern was appreciated—although I knew she had another motive as well.

Living with Judy meant there was very little chance of Roger showing up with a last-minute proposal. My sister wanted to keep him from hurting me again.

Feeling abandoned, lonely, and sad, I agreed. However, I didn't let my apartment go. I wanted to make sure I had a place of my own to return to when I felt stronger.

I loved a lot of things about the upstairs bedroom I moved into next to my niece. Knowing it was my favorite color, Judy had painted it a robin's egg blue. She had also purchased a navy-blue bedspread covered in little white flowers that complemented a small white chest of drawers with a matching nightstand. Several pictures of Michele were displayed on top.

One of my favorite aspects of the room was its little balcony that overlooked a backyard filled with red, orange, yellow, purple, and pink flowers of different varieties in the summer, and golden mums and autumn foliage in the fall. The yard even had a carriage house from days-gone-by. Photos of old buildings and families who had lived in the area were hung on the walls of the carriage house. Like most of the houses on Main Street, Adamstown, my sister's big, two-story home, with stained glass windows and rich, dark wood, echoed the historical era it came from.

As I waited to give birth, this peaceful sanctuary allowed me to think and just be, especially when the weather cooled, and my November delivery date approached. I often bundled up and slipped on a pair of gloves so I could sit outside with my hot morning tea. I found the crisp air exhilarating and enjoyed watching my breath blow tendrils of smoky fog toward the sky. When the birds chattered and the wind whipped Judy's freshly washed linens on the line, I'd rub my swollen belly and allow myself to dream. Would I have a boy or girl? What would he/she look like? How would Roger react?

Cathartic Release

Back in February, Mom had mailed me a writing journal for my birthday, encouraging me to record my daily thoughts, even if only in a few lines. In the past, I found Mom's attempts at "fixing me" irritating. But I had to admit, receiving mail with her written tidbits, recipes, pictures, and reports from Indianapolis made my days more interesting. She explained how writing was therapeutic for her, and said she found it liberating and freeing. I wasn't yet privy to just how much she needed that cathartic release. The shoebox effect ran deep in my family.

Perhaps it will help you, too, Mom told me in her letter, referencing the journal.

I decided to give it a try and discovered she was right. Expressing my thoughts and feelings in words "for my eyes only" did make me feel better. It also made it easier to review my past, process my present, and prepare for my future.

On a chilly, November morning in 1978, I'd slept in, but was instantly wide-awake and alert when the first pains of labor shot across the lower part of my abdomen. I peeled the navy bedspread back and proceeded to stand up when another pain hit. I started toward the stairs to tell Jute, but warm liquid trickling down the insides of both my legs stopped me. Frightened, I called for her.

"Sissy," I cried, "Sissy, come here, I need you." (As an adult, I never called Judy, Sissy, unless I was hurt or in pain.) I repeated myself again, then exhaled in relief when I heard her running up the steps

Judy's soothing voice was all I needed. "It's okay honey. Your water's just broken," she said calmly. "Sissy's here. It's going to be all right."

Because Gary only worked fifteen minutes from home, Judy had taken him to work in the mornings over the past week, so she could have access to their only car. She'd also arranged babysitting for Michele. My sister had planned out every detail.

Helping me down the stairwell, Judy said, "I need to get the car, but first, I have to call your doctor and let him know we're on our way to the hospital." She gingerly assisted, as I sat down in a kitchen chair.

Judy called the doctor, then hurried outside to get the car and back it onto the street. It only took a couple of minutes before she ran back inside and appeared with my suitcase. Once she settled me onto the front seat of the car, Judy scurried around and got in the driver's seat. One punch of the gas, and we were off.

It's Time

I watched trees, sidewalks, and houses whiz by as Judy sped for the hospital. When we approached and passed Roger's place, I used my peripheral vision to see how my sister might react. If she noticed, she never let on.

By the time we reached the hospital, it was nearly 10:00 a.m. When I was taken back to a room, Jute stayed with me. She tried to make light conversation, and sprinkled praise amidst her attempts to distract and encourage me.

"You're doing so well, Mace. We might get to see our one o'clock story after all," she said, mentioning our favorite soap opera.

But I could tell she was just trying to be strong for me. Several times, she left the room and reappeared with red eyes. She'd obviously been crying.

I was prepared for the kind of long labor I'd had with Michele, so when the nurse checked me at noon and said, "You're ready," I was caught off-guard. Months of pent-up emotions spilled onto my face.

Jute tried to reassure me, but I'd dreaded this moment of giving birth without my baby's father at my side. My sister kissed my forehead and cheeks in between terms of endearment. "You'll be okay, honey. Don't worry, Sissy's here."

I caught movement out of the corner of my eye.

"It's time," a voice said. "You'll have to stay here," the nurse said to Judy.

"But I need her with me," I pleaded.

"I'm sorry, but no one else is allowed in delivery," the nurse said firmly.

The last thing I remember before the anesthesia wiped away my conscious thoughts, was tasting the salt of mixed tears—mine and Judy's. My sister had to wait outside.

Later, Judy told me she stood in the hallway and watched a nurse come out with Jesse. My daughter was crying as the nurse walked briskly away. After Jesse was carried off, they let Judy see me very briefly, but I was hysterical and screaming for my child. The nurse told my sister she would give me some medicine to calm me, but Judy couldn't handle my pain. She said she fled before the meds had time to kick in. Not until long after my sister's death, would I find out why this affected her so much.

A Beautiful Gesture

When I woke up, Judy was gone, my child was gone, Roger was absent, and I was furious. This is when I let loose on the nurse—demanding to see my child. I learned my daughter entered the world at 1:08 p.m.

Poor Gabe, the kind orderly the nurse delegated to deal with my wrath, took most of my blistering emotional heat. But he also received initial credit for a beautiful gesture—credit that belonged to someone else. It all started with a mistake.

The evening after I delivered Jessica, the door to my hospital room swung open. I looked up and locked eyes with a familiar face. Three steps in, Roger's cousin froze where he stood. "Marcie? Oh, hey. Um, I thought this was someone else's room. How are you?"

Thinking Roger sent him to snoop on me, I felt a little miffed. If the father of my child wanted to know something about her or me, he should have been man enough to come find out for himself. "I'm fine. Tired. Having a baby does that to you," I retorted.

"Uh, yeah. Well, sorry. I didn't mean to bother you. See ya later." Roger's cousin quickly left the room.

The physical and emotional cost of the day had already drained me. Roger's cousin's mistake exhausted me even more. It didn't take long after his departure for me to fall fast asleep.

The next morning, I carefully pushed myself out of the bed to use the restroom. I didn't see it when I got up, but afterward, as I lay back down, I saw a single, red rose on the stand. I thought of Gabe's gentleness the afternoon before and smiled. *That was thoughtful.*

Gabe came to check on me when his shift started, so I said, "Thank you for the rose. It's beautiful."

A look of confusion spread across his face. "What rose?"

Now it was my turn to look and sound confused. "You didn't leave a rose on my nightstand?"

"No," he said. "Maybe you have a secret admirer."

I was sure that was not the case. Years later, when Roger and I reunited, he confessed that after accidentally walking into my room, his cousin called him upon leaving the hospital. A little while later, Roger arrived and cracked the door open, unsure if I would receive him. Seeing I was asleep, he simply slipped in and left the rose he'd brought on the nightstand.

I never knew he showed up. But this was a Roger habit—tiny, random acts of kindness, to ease his guilt after he'd been a jerk.

Shoebox Memories

When I got out of the hospital, Jute told me to stay with her as long as I wanted. So other than exchanging clothes from my closet or drawers and checking my mail, I lived with my sister and her family instead of at my place. I was glad I wouldn't have to be all alone on Thanksgiving and Christmas. But I did spend December 31, 1978 by myself. It was New Year's Eve and I had no one to share the arrival of 1979 with.

Michele was with her dad on the farm, Judy and Gary went to a friend's party, my niece was at a sleepover, Roger was with who knew who or where, and my baby was with strangers. I decided I may as well go home and sleep in my own bed.

At my apartment, I ran a hot bath, turned my stereo on in the living room, then went back to the bathroom, undressed, and stepped in to the tub. I loved my Calgon soaks—the blue water softened my skin and the satiny scent calmed my soul. They always reminded me of the sisterly times Jute and I shared when we were teens, where one bathed and the other sat on the vanity, as we talked and solved all the world's problems.

Extending my body fully under the water, I stretched out. Then I reflected back in time to the year before. How things had changed since New Year's Eve, 1977.

It had all felt so magical, my New Year of firsts with Roger. My first black dress. The first grown up dance I attended. My first taste of true freedom. The first time Roger said, "I love you."

But now, the song on the stereo reminded me I needed to take my life in a new direction. Remembering Dr. Stanley's directive to "pretend you never gave birth," I considered how I would go on without my daughter while trying to heal my broken heart. I could not imagine the doctor was right. How would this painful time ever pass?

To survive, I had to repress my thoughts about Jesse, or I would go nuts. Recalling the shoebox where I'd stored all of the tangible reminders of her birth, I decided to fill another box, a metaphorical shoebox, with my memories. I would hide Jesse's existence in the recesses of my mind.

I swished water and thought about the common question strangers often asked. "How many children do you have?"

Laying in the silky, blue water, I resolved to make my answer, "One daughter."

I was afraid if I didn't, I might totally lose my mind. Then, in order to preserve my sanity, I focused my brain elsewhere—and practiced my re-scripted truth.

I turned my mind to typical new year thoughts: making better choices, eating healthier, finding new friends, and deciding on a career path. I even practiced answering out loud, "One daughter," to get used to conversations I never wanted to have.

I got lost in my thoughts and became hypnotized by the sound of blue water trickling through my fingertips. The stereo kept me from hearing the doorbell.

Change of Heart

The next morning, I pulled out my journal, paperclipped several painful pages together, skipped some blanks, then began documenting the next chapter of my life over a cup of tea. After I finished writing, I dressed, grabbed my coat, and headed out for the morning walk that would launch me into my new health initiative. Once outside the door, I saw the gray Olds parked next to the curb.

I felt the hood as I approached the driver's side door. It was cool to the touch, this meant the car had sat, unmoving, for hours. Roger was passed out cold, behind the wheel.

I knocked sharply on the window.

Roger jumped at the sound and looked at me with bloodshot eyes. When he rolled the window down, a wave of alcohol and morning breath wafted toward me. "Happy New Year. Hop in," he greeted, as if nothing sad had ever happened between us.

I should have told him to drop dead. I had a choice. I should have run inside my house and locked the door so Roger couldn't manipulate me. Instead, I did exactly as he dictated. I got in.

Roger only drove a few blocks before he parked beneath a grove of oak trees, whose stripped bare branches danced in the winter wind. The fabric on the seat squeaked when he turned to face me.

"Marcie, I messed up. Bad. I was a coward. I know I made a mistake."

When he suddenly slammed his fist against the dashboard and cursed himself, I stiffened. But the combination of his bright, blue eyes glistening with tears, and the tender way he reached for my hand, made me relax.

"I abandoned you, Marcie, and I'm so sorry. I wish I could take it all back. I'm a screw up."

Roger lowered his shoulders and they slumped forward. He looked at my hands instead of into my eyes when he said, "I just wanted you to know I've been thinking about all of this. I know you're hurting, but I'm hurting, too."

My head spun as I listened in awe.

Roger continued. "People make mistakes. Don't they? Can we get her back? I never signed off on anything."

This was my dream coming true. My brain disregarded any warnings, instead I focused on the hope in Roger's change of heart.

The next morning, I called Dr. Stanley's office. He did not take my call, nor did he return it. After several attempts over multiple days, Roger and I, united, walked into Dr. Stanley's office unannounced. We demanded to speak with the physician.

With a sour expression and dismissive tone, the nurse said, "Dr.

Stanley has patients and is not available to speak with you about this matter right now. You can wait if you like."

We waited. Hour after slow-motion hour, the hands rounded the numbers on the clock. Finally, a few minutes before the office was due to close, the doctor invited us back to his office. But he did not welcome our inquiry.

"It's too late. Marcie already signed the contract," Dr. Stanley said as if he were discussing the sale of a used car.

"But I don't even have a copy of what I signed," I protested.

Agitated, Dr. Stanley said, "It's a closed, private adoption, remember? We talked about this." Roger stood up, rage racking his body. "But she's my daughter, too. I didn't sign anything. Don't I get a say in my child's life?"

Dr. Stanley raised his voice to nearly match Roger's decibel. "Mr. Roth, though I understand your emotions in this matter, my hands are tied. There is nothing further I can do. You should have taken action when you had the opportunity."

The doctor got up from his chair and walked to his office door and opened it. With a gentler tone he said, "I suggest you take my earlier advice to Marcie, forget you had a child and move on with your life. This will pass in time."

The finality of his statement sunk in to both of us. Dejected and broken, Roger grabbed my hand and led me out the door. Our little girl was lost to us—we had been defeated.

A New Chapter

Though we'd failed to get our daughter back, Roger pushed for a reconciliation. But our relationship had many strikes against it. As much as I loved him, I could not forgive him. Roger's presence was a daily reminder of what I'd lost, and that his absence during my pregnancy had allowed it to happen. I broke up with him a few weeks after the incident in Dr. Stanley's office.

Hoping to help me heal my hurting heart, Judy fixed me up with a friend of hers. Though it didn't work out, her well-intentioned pressure did launch me into a new chapter of my life. I enrolled in college, cut my long hair and had it styled in a fashionable short do, and began to date. I even landed a great job, getting hired at Merrill Lynch. But Roger wasn't entirely out of the picture.

Several of my dates were ruined, when Roger tailed us and made a scene. I felt a strange mix of anger and pride that he still wanted me that much. But as Judy and I drove to Southern Indiana to attend our grandfather's funeral, we talked things through. I realized how unhealthy my feelings were. If I wanted Michele and I to have the life we deserved, I needed to get my life fully in order. Though it stung, I knew that meant no Roger. I would have to rid myself of the unexplainable power he held over me.

While in Indianapolis, Mom encouraged me to move there.

"But I don't want to leave Judy," I said. "Besides, I finally have a job I love."

"You two can visit each other," Mom said. "And you could transfer to the Merrill Lynch office in downtown Indy. I'll get you the number." She opened a drawer and pilfered inside, pulling out the phone book.

A few minutes later, I was talking to the office manager.

Mom and my stepfather drove to Pennsylvania in a truck, loaded Michele and me up, and moved us into our new lives. Though I forced myself not to look back, a piece of my heart tugged hard as we pulled away. I would miss the close proximity of my sister—and I was not over Roger.

We arrived in the spring of 1982. Indianapolis represented the shedding of past wounds and the creation of a brand new me. I walked into the Indy Merrill Lynch office with goals and an attitude to back it up. I would work hard, build my career, and keep my social calendar full. I would bury my shoebox so deep that even I couldn't dig it out. This was how I would beat the demons. No one would know the truth.

As I'd done the day I got home from the hospital, when I'd chosen the box to place Jesse's mementos in, I decided to selectively store my true emotions away during that season of my life. Have you ever spent time and energy trying to remove something from your memory?

It worked for a long time, but once a box gets full, something's bound to spill out. For years, I kept insanely doing the same things over and over again, hoping for different results. I would have to learn there are consequences for keeping a shoebox full of emotional pain, even when you hide it behind a shield of success.

UNPACKING YOUR SHOEBOX

The Shoebox Sherpa's Points to Ponder

- Review your life-altering events via journaling. Often, any residual, unresolved grief can be unearthed via remembering through writing, fully freeing you to deal with your past pain and releasing you from its grip.

- As hard as it is, ask people you trust to give you their honest feedback about decisions you've made or are about to make, and consequences they imagine. The truth sometimes hurts, but it can save you from increasing emotional pain.

- If you've packed and hidden a shoebox, tangible or emotional, pull it off the shelf. You don't have to take the lid off just yet, but acknowledging its existence is a huge first step to freedom.

1. Is there anything you've left unattended that still bothers you today—if you allow yourself to think about it? Could you still pursue a resolution?

_____

_____

_____

_____

2. Have you ever made a fresh start somewhere, hoping for a clean slate that would allow you to leave part of your past behind? How did it work out? _____

_____

_____

_____

_____

CHAPTER TEN

SHIELD OF SUCCESS

If you've ever experienced trauma, loss, or abuse of any kind, you understand the drive to save yourself from the feelings attached to them. Stuffing our emotions is an instinctual reaction to painful experiences. But human instinct is not always healthy or good—especially on the heels of deep hurt.

Have you ever buried memories or tried to hide your past in the shoebox effect? If so, did it seem to work for a while, maybe even for years, only to haunt you with a growing force you eventually could no longer deny?

After being coerced into surrendering my daughter and failing at a reconciliation attempt with Roger, I set my sights on something I felt I could control—my ability to affect and help others. It became a career focus, but I recognized this gift at a young age.

I was eighteen years old when I first realized I had a talent for influencing people. While married to my ex-husband, Bill, we spent many Sundays at his family's farm. Along with his other siblings and their spouses, we were expected for dinner each week—no excuses. Table conversations were mostly led by the men, but the women were free to join in at any time. One particular meal stands out in my mind—my husband and I nearly turned the table upside down.

The men were discussing how women working outside of the home had changed the dynamics of the family. Remember, this was the mid-seventies, and as with other major cultural shifts, opinions on both sides were strong.

Bill said smugly, "A woman's place is in the home. No wife of mine is getting a job."

My husband's proud boasting triggered thoughts of my daddy, who had made similar statements many times. I'm not sure where his thinking came from, because it did not come from Daddy's mom—we called her Nanny.

Nanny was a sassy, bold, and proud woman born in 1900, who worked her entire life and outlived three husbands. My Aunt Helen, Daddy's sister, must have gotten her independent way of thinking from her mother. Both women were born before their time. They were strong females who worked outside the home and expected their husbands to help them with daily chores such as grocery shopping and bathing their children. I guess I had just enough of my Nanny in me.

When I heard Bill say his wife wasn't getting a job, my internal reaction was swift. I suppressed the urge to reach across and smack him with a piece of my mother-in-law's roast beef. Out of respect for the rest of Bill's family, I exercised great restraint to keep my thoughts to myself. But mentally, I let him have it.

Who does he think he is anyway? He's not my father. I'm an adult woman and I take orders from no man. If I choose to work outside of our home, I will. I glared at Bill. No wife of his is working outside the home? Really? Well, *no wife of yours is giving you sex tonight, either.*

My mother-in-law at the time, Nina, a mother of six, was both perceptive and a peacemaker. She must have seen the glint in my green eyes as I shot Bill the look of death, because she abruptly ended the conversation by standing up and asking me for help in the kitchen.

A True Ally

Nina had witnessed many of my acid tongue lashings with Bill. I think she understood my desperation for a fight with her son; this was the period where I desperately tried debate tactics to get a reaction from him. Of course, it never worked. However, I found Nina loving, and she was a true ally.

She took my hand and patted it. "I'll help you get a job," she said with a warm smile. "I know just what to say to Bill." She handed me several pieces of her homemade blackberry custard pie to carry in for dessert. Then she winked. "Just keep it between us."

As always, I marveled at Nina's ability to quietly move minds and hearts. And true to her word, Nina came through. The following week I was sitting across the desk from Mr. Amato, interviewing for a cashier's position at a local department store.

I immediately liked his cheery personality, warm smile, and how he always seemed to talk with his hands. His thick, Italian accent made me think of *The Godfather*, the book I'd read on the bus from Indiana several months before.

Mr. Amato was looking for a new cashier and offered me the job on the spot. I loved the way he pronounced my name without the r. "Maahcie, you can start tomorrow."

Line of Questioning

I was born in Southern Indiana near the Kentucky border, across the river from Louisville, but until I went to work, I wasn't aware that my dialect sounded much different from the Pennsylvanians in the area. However, when several customers asked me where I was from and what brought me to PA, I caught on. Apparently, I had a slight southern drawl that made people think I was from the deep south. I soon picked up the nickname, Kentuckiana. I actually liked it.

I found it easy to talk to strangers and meet new people. Soon, my customers waved and called me by name as they entered the store. Often, the regulars waited longer just to check out in my lane, and it didn't go unnoticed. Mr. Amato picked up on something I had not yet learned about myself.

He walked up to me with a smile in his eyes. "How would you-a like to work-a in the record department? You like music-a, right?"

"I love music," I said.

"Perfect. Sales are down in that department, and we need-a someone with your ability to connect with people, to help-a pick sales back up. You'd also unpack and display 45s and albums, keep everything-a clean and organized, and assist customers in making purchases. Are you interested?"

I jumped at the offer. Soon, I was happily guiding customers to the checkout line, stacks of records in their hands.

One day Mr. Amato called me into his office. My mind raced. *Am I getting fired? What did I do wrong? Is it because I'm pregnant now?* I instinctively reached down and stroked my belly, where my first child was just revealing its baby bump.

When I sat down, my manager immediately began grilling me. I was confused by his line of questioning.

"Do you-a enjoy working here, Maahcie?" he said.

"Oh, yes," I said.

In his thick Italian accent, he said, "What are your-a future plans? After your-a baby is born?"

"I hadn't given it much thought," I said, touching my belly protectively. "I'd like to return to work as soon as possible after it gets here. If that's okay." I had only been working in the record department for three months and now felt uneasy. Maybe I wasn't doing as well as I'd thought.

Mr. Amato pulled a report out of his desk. "I thought we should-a review your-a progress, and see if you have any comments, suggestions, or questions."

I held my breath for a few seconds after he handed me his sales report. I glanced at the ledger, but wasn't sure what all of the numbers meant.

"Don't worry, I will-a explain everything," he said. Then he detailed the figures and percentages. "Your sales are moving in a positive direction. This is the first time I've seen them go up in a long-a time." He pointed to several red circles, arrows, and numbers—and he sounded pleased.

I felt thrilled.

"What do you need from me to help you?" he said.

I paused for only a brief moment. An idea had been brewing in my mind for several weeks, but I'd been too afraid to ask Mr. Amato about it. I took a deep breath and bravely spoke. "A record player," I said. "I need a record player in my department."

He looked at me inquisitively before responding. "That's a-easy. We sell-a those in the electronics department," he said. "But why would-a we need to move one to the record area?"

My heart pounded. I had rehearsed my reasoning a dozen times, so I knew exactly what to say. "How can we expect our customers to buy something they haven't heard? Or what if they've heard a song they like, but don't know the name of it? If we can play the songs in the store for our customers, I believe they'll want to take more records home."

Mr. Amato nodded in slow agreement, as if processing. Then his eyes widened. "The power of suggestion. Bellissimo. Let's do it."

I had never heard the term, "power of suggestion" before. I had bought records since I was old enough to earn an allowance, and I knew what made me buy. But when it came to sales, I was young, green, and unpolished. I was only following intuition.

Sitting across from Mr. Amato, I acted like an authority on the subject and agreed with him. "Exactly." I said. "And if a customer asks about the player, I can always call Steve in electronics to come over, right? Maybe we could make two sales instead of just one."

Mr. Amato grinned. He reached for his phone and spoke into the intercom. I heard his voice overhead. "Steve, please-a come to the manager's office immediately."

I relaxed in the stiff office chair—feeling satisfied. Mr. Amato liked my idea.

Within six weeks, sales in the record department increased 52%. I got a raise and praise from Mr. Amato. Also in that time, I referred customers to Steve for to purchase record players and stereos. After eight referrals to Steve, I got another raise, and a discount on my first stereo system. I experienced an incredible high from that success, and I wanted more. A seed sprouted and grew, but it had been planted years earlier—by my stepmother, Marge. Later, my mother nurtured it.

Secret Language

Dad and Marge seemed to have more of a practical relationship than a romantic one. She was a divorced secretary, employed at the same chemical company where Daddy worked. A year after my mom left, Daddy married Marge, but she didn't arrive alone. I instantly became a big sister to Marge's daughter, and it was wonderful.

When I was in high school, Marge advised I go to college, or at the very least, to take classes that would provide me with skills or a trade. Her thinking was different from Daddy's, who appeared uninterested in higher education. I often wondered if he was a little intimidated or embarrassed for not graduating like his older brother, Bob. Instead Daddy chose to quit school and join the service. He eventually became a World War II veteran.

While trying to make up my mind about attending college, I tried to talk to Daddy in hopes of getting his insights about which direction I should take.

Instead of wisdom, he barked at me. "Made it just fine without a college degree. You don't look hungry." He pointed to the ceiling, "There's a roof over your head, right?"

But Marge provided the gentle guidance I needed.

"You should take typing. It can open all kinds of doors for you," she urged. Marge knew this from her own experiences. She was a fast typist and still utilized her shorthand skills for efficiency as well as additional income.

Every day, at least one of her many lists lay on the kitchen table next to our AM/FM radio. Marge would make to-do lists in shorthand while she listened to the news. The squiggles made absolutely no sense to me at all. It was like she knew her own secret language. I wanted to learn it as well, so she graciously agreed to teach me.

Many evenings, Marge and I would sit under the maple tree in our back yard. After she patiently checked my math, especially my educational nemesis, fractions, we would move on to shorthand. Timing me, Marge taught me to transcribe as she dictated. When we finished, she would read the secret scrawl and check it for accuracy.

Then, as part of our ritual, we went back inside the house, where she would sit me down at her typewriter. Marge watched me carefully, as I transferred my shorthand into typewritten text. These were the days before word processors and home computers, so everything was done manually. I loved hearing the click of the keys and the ding that alerted me it was time to throw the carriage. Marge instilled both work ethics and discipline in me—she is the reason behind any of my work success—as is Judy.

Successful Longshot

Years after I'd grown the record sales at Mr. Amato's department store, my sister, Jute, saw an ad in the newspaper for a company called Merrill Lynch. She encouraged me to respond. Circled in my niece's deep purple Crayola, the paper read, *Wire Operator Wanted. Must be able to type 90 WPM.*

"Check this out Mace," she said eagerly. This is right up your alley."

Only half-listening at first, I said, "Merrill who? What's that?"

Judy showed me the ad, and it did sound like something I could do. Thanks to Marge, I knew how to type, and type fast, so I called the number listed.

The person on the phone immediately set up an interview with the manager, Lou Elias. I went in the next day.

Mr. Elias gave me a series of exercises to complete. The first and most important was to check my speed and accuracy. Scared to death and intimidated by all the "suits" and college degrees, I thought I was in over my head and felt like a phony. *What does Merrill Lynch want with a scrawny, high school graduate with little experience like me?*

Lou sensed my anxiety. "Relax, Marcie."

Relax? He was standing over my shoulder and watching me. I thought I would throw up.

But then I closed my eyes and took a deep breath, before imagining myself back with Marge, sitting at her typewriter. My fingers began to move, slow at first, and then they picked up speed, until they flew across the keys.

After ten minutes, Lou clicked his stopwatch. "Time," he said, letting me know it was over.

I exhaled loudly and sat back.

Proofing my work, I heard him say under his breath, "Not bad. Not bad, at all. You averaged 92 WPM and you've done so accurately. Welcome to Merrill Lynch."

I couldn't believe that was all it took to get the job.

Years later, when I transferred to the Indianapolis location, Lou and the office threw me a big "Best of Luck" party, sending me off with my own briefcase and Cross Pen. Lou pulled me aside and gave me a card with a $100 bill inside. The message in the card put a proud smile on my face. *To Marcie, my most successful longshot. Best of luck in Indy. Knock 'em dead!*

The foundation of Marge's structured discipline, Judy's belief in me, and Lou's initial encouragement at Merrill Lynch, set the stage for a thirty-two-year, financial career. And where they left off, my mother picked up. Finally having me in her home after years of separation, she cheered me on as I obtained my Series7 Securities license in 1986 and was promoted to Operations Manager in 1987.

After fifteen years with Merrill Lynch, I left and went into banking. I was one of the top officers, earned additional sales and insurance licenses, and became a training officer for new manager recruits. I received the Winners' and President's Circle Award and won five-star trips to places like Mexico and Bermuda for exceeding sales goals. But my happiness was a surface response.

I came to call these years my Shield of Success. The highs of career achievement helped me protect my secret and kept me covered with distraction. But you can only conceal something, even from yourself, for so long. Eventually you get tired of holding the facade in place, especially when triggers and sabotage come.

A Shield of Success pushes your shoebox further back on the shelf of your mind—but it cannot make it disappear. Guilt, shame, unworthiness, and more all wait to pop the top off and reveal the secrets hidden inside. As I found out, eventually your past will force its way into your present.

UNPACKING YOUR SHOEBOX

The Shoebox Sherpa's Points to Ponder

- If you feel past memories beginning to bubble up, instinct says shove the lid down tighter. But releasing your past into your conscious mind is the way to improve your present. Don't let fear and anxiety keep you emotionally imprisoned.

- There's nothing wrong with success—it's a beautiful thing. But don't fall prey to the belief that career success can replace personal peace. True, inner fulfillment comes from allowing yourself to experience balance in all aspects of life.

- Just as your job skills are something to be proud of, so are coping skills such as bravery, tenacity, authenticity, and integrity.

1. What have you used to shield yourself from feeling pain? Work? Romantic relationships? Money? Possessions? Travel? Sarcasm? Emotional aloofness? Arrogance? Timidity?

   _____

   _____

   _____

   _____

2. Is there a person who pointed you in the right direction and changed the course of your life for the better? Have you been intentional to thank them? _____

   _____

   _____

   _____

   _____

CHAPTER ELEVEN

TRIGGERS AND SABOTAGE

When you can no longer hide from the unresolved grief, secrets, and lies placed in your shoebox, there's only one recourse. When triggers and self-sabotage have wreaked enough havoc, you realize there's only one way to reduce the pressure. When you've tried everything to escape the past, but memories still haunt you in your dreams, there's only one alternative.

Face your pain!

If you've ever tried the shoebox effect, you've likely grappled with intense anxiety or depression. Only a professional can diagnose you, but you might even struggle with the effects of PTSD. I wrestled all of these symptoms and more.

I didn't find everything I hoped for when I nudged the lid off my metaphorical shoebox, but I did discover a lot of healing. That first action step made me feel like I might implode at times, but I'm so thankful I pushed through. The anxiety I felt the first day I began the official search for my daughter, Jessie, caused a swirl of questions.

Haven't I waited long enough? It's been twenty-nine years of wondering and daydreaming, why do I feel so afraid of looking now? And where do I start?

I did not yet know how brainwashed or gaslighted I'd become on the subject of adoption. Over the years, to keep my sanity and ability to function, I transformed into the "good birthmother." Compliant, I asked no questions and pretended I'd never given my flesh and blood child away. When people asked me how many children I had, I answered as I'd practiced, "I have one daughter."

I'd developed myself as the "consummate actress," under the pressures to suppress my emotions and never tell. Dr. Stanley's goal became mine—keep the secret silent. And I accomplished it. There was just one problem, I lost important pieces of the real me as I lived life from a virtual stage. Self-sabotage slithered in without me realizing it was there.

I punished myself in big and small ways for becoming the calloused mother who gave her baby away. I avoided reading magazine articles or watching anything on TV associated with adoption. I masterfully pushed my memories into the deepest closets in my brain, but occasionally, the old fear slipped out.

Even the slightest interest in adoption, reunifications, or something as simple as a baby shower, made me worry my secret would be found out. So, I feigned an aloof disinterest and avoided anything associated with mothers and children. To this day, the sound of any infant's cry can send me out of a room.

Reconnected

Decades after the surrender of our daughter had torn us apart, Roger re-entered my life once again. We were first reconnected by a simple phone call right after the death of Dreyfus in September of 2007. After that, we started talking every night at 7:00, and continued until the wee hours of the morning. For weeks, I ran on adrenaline and the thought of "us" again.

In December, Roger invited me out to Pennsylvania the week after Christmas, so we could spend New Year's Eve together. Reflecting back to 1977 and 1978, I thought it could go either way—fantastically wonderful or a complete disaster.

After her divorce, Judy was living with me in 2007, and wanted to go see her daughter MaryBeth anyway, so we decided to make the trip together. We packed up Jute's SUV and headed east. I loved traveling with my sister. She was a great storyteller and tease. I laughed the whole way, making the long, six-hundred-mile drive seem shorter.

The plan was to arrive in Adamstown around 12:30 a.m., check into our motel, and get a good night's rest. I would call Roger in the morning, and the three of us would meet for breakfast.

True to our schedule, we arrived at 12:15 and checked in to our room. However, the excitement running through me could not be contained. There was no way I could wait until tomorrow morning to see Roger. After all, it had been twenty-nine years since we had last laid eyes on one another. But mixed with my anticipation, I developed a big case of nerves.

We had both aged, put on a few pounds, and were now grown adults. What if we didn't like each other? What if we didn't have anything in common other than memories of our youth? What if it was like going on the worst blind date you could imagine?

Judy had changed as well. She knew how much I had suffered and longed for a resolution with Roger. She also believed he couldn't possibly be the same playboy he had been decades before. Finally, I had my sister's approval to move forward. "Call him, Mace. You've waited long enough."

And I had waited. I had also dreamed of this moment for years. Now I would see him again, be held in his arms again, and experience that feeling of pure bliss I had the first time he kissed me. Could things still be the same between us? I had to know.

I rushed to shower and put on the new outfit I'd carefully chosen. Jute did my hair, then I made the phone call. Just as I hoped, Roger did not want to wait either. Within twenty minutes, I was in his arms again. It was if I had never left—only now we had a new mission.

Roger had planned our New Year's Eve celebration to the minute. We went to a party where many of our old friends who'd heard of my visit were attending. It was great seeing everyone and telling our story about plans to search for our daughter.

Never married, or having fathered other children, Roger could not contain himself about the thought of actually being a dad. We ate, drank, talked, danced, and enjoyed ourselves, but as 11:30 approached, Roger appeared with my red coat and leopard spotted gloves. "Let's go," he said with a big grin on his face. "I have a surprise for you." I thought it rather odd to leave a New Year's party before midnight, but I was intrigued.

Arm in arm, Roger and I exited the party and made our way through crunching snow. A few minutes into the drive, I knew where he was taking me, and I had to smile to myself. This was so Roger.

He pulled the car into a parking spot at our old hangout, the Adamstown Rod and Gun Club, a place full of good times and memories. I instantly remembered dances and long board tournaments, officer's meetings, kids' fishing rodeos on the lake, picnics in the pavilion, and euchre.

Only now, unlike twenty-nine years ago, there was no dance, though the place had not changed much. The club was fully decorated for the holidays as before, the great pine in the corner dominating the empty dance floor.

Roger ordered drinks and we found an empty table. As it neared midnight, I watched him as he got up and placed some coins in the jukebox. Smiling broadly, he took my hand in his and led me to the empty dance floor. I closed my eyes and rested my head on his shoulder as the familiar piano melody I loved so well began to play. We swayed to Floyd Kramer's, "Last Date."

He remembered.

My face washed fresh with tears as violins pulled me softly back in time. I imagined us young and in love again—that hot, sweaty, crazy love where you constantly long for one another. I cried for all the lost years we could have had as a family. I cried for Jessica. I cried for all three of us.

The song ended and midnight fell. Just as he had thirty years before, Roger cupped my face with both hands and gently kissed me. "Happy New Year." He pulled back, a serious expression on his features. "I know this sounds crazy, but you were the one. I know I hurt you and broke your heart. But, say yes. Say you'll marry me. Neither of us is getting any younger."

Four months later, Roger and I were wed in Indiana. We immediately began the search for our daughter, only this time, we were married and had a more stable foundation. Roger gave me the push of confidence I needed to type my first query. After I hit the enter button, I sat back in shock. Seconds later, my computer screen lit up like Vegas at midnight.

What in the world?

Escaping My Demons

My eyes widened with disbelief as I scrolled through the search engine results. Hundreds of ads and agencies offered to help me "Find your lost loved one." I opened various links to websites—most wanted money I didn't have. If one looked credible, however, I posted a message to briefly tell my story and explain my dilemma. I felt desperate to find my daughter but had no idea where to go for real help.

Roger's renewed presence in my life provided strength and gave me courage to wade through the internet almost daily. He allowed me to cry about the loss, vent about how it affected my life, and listened to why I wanted to search. It didn't matter if others said it made no sense—it made sense to me. Roger understood where I was coming from. Jessica was his daughter, too.

I had no fantasies or unreasonable expectations about what I'd discover when I found Jesse. I assumed she had an amazing life, based on the description Dr. Stanley had given me of the family he arranged the private adoption for. I never assumed she'd want to know me or dig into her true identity. I validated my belief system with the fact that she hadn't looked for me.

I had no plans to interfere in Jesse's life. If she chose to let me know her, I would rejoice. If she rejected me, well, I was practiced at that already.

I simply wanted to step off the stage of lies and shame I'd built, drop the consummate actress facade, and walk with my head up. The truth would allow me to breathe freely. Finally, I could escape all the demons that had haunted me for decades. Or could I?

Looking back, I was ill-prepared for what lie ahead. It was like skipping high school and going straight to college at age thirteen. I lacked emotional maturity for the situation. I did not even understand the basics about the complexity of adoption. I was just a mother grieving for her lost child. I would soon discover that adoption has as many layers as a Vidalia onion.

Missing Pieces

Adoption has many aspects to it: political arenas, social projections, human interest, legal landmines, civil etiquette, and emotional surprises. Just when you think you know everything, another layer suddenly appears—then another, and another, and another. Finding my daughter meant learning and experiencing all of these facets. I needed more than sheer luck to find Jessica—I needed a miracle.

The general public's understanding of the adoption system is not accurate. Most people believe adoptions are nothing but pure bliss and unrestrained joy. Adopting a child is marketed as smiling faces and saving the little one from poverty or abuse. Sometimes birthmothers are painted as having no compassion, throwing their children away like an old pair of shoes.

Many adoptive families don't recognize the past the child they bring into their home to raise as their own brings. They don't understand there's a history, a piece of themselves the child was forced to leave behind. To the adoptive family, the child's life began with them. As long as they provide love and security, they believe the child can fully become their own, happily forgetting they originated somewhere else. In rare cases this might happen, but most people ache to know about their missing pieces.

Adoption usually begins as a loss or trauma for the baby. The child does not come to the new family with a clean slate, as some agencies use as a selling ploy. They have a past that belongs to them and needs to be acknowledged and respected.

I knew none of this in the spring of 2008, shortly into my marriage to Jesse's birth father. On Father's Day 2008, as I'd done many times over the past several months, I sat down at my computer—both terrified and excited to open my emotional shoe box. For twenty-nine years, Jesse's last cries had haunted me. I was no longer young and naïve. I was ready to take ownership of my choices.

I breathed deep, adjusted my body in the office chair, and began to type. My hands shook and my palms sweated. As always, I feared that by simply typing the words of my story on a search screen, anyone and everyone would have access to my secret. It felt like the whole world was peering into my past. I feared stroking those black keys would unleash years of shame, and all of it would descend upon me. I wasn't familiar with the term "trauma triggers" yet. But in spite of the cloud of emotions swirling inside me, I typed on.

An hour later, I stared motionlessly at the screen, feeling overwhelmed and exhausted after another round of posts on various sites. I sighed and turned the machine off. My daughter, Michele, her kids, and me, were taking Roger out for a Father's Day lunch. I needed the mental escape of relaxing as a family.

Lunch worked. We had a great time, and it helped me forget all about my angst from the morning. The only thing that invaded my peace was the strange number that incessantly tried to get me to answer my cell phone.

After a few hours, we arrived back home where our dogs, Cooley and Cody, raced to the patio door, anxious to go out. The house phone began to ring as soon as I'd closed the door after freeing the dogs to play and relieve themselves. I glanced at the caller ID. Not recognizing the number, I almost didn't answer it. It was Sunday, I wanted to ignore it like I had my cell. Some decisions, however, change everything about your life.

Search Angel

I heard a stranger's voice—female. The caller seemed anxious to identify herself.

"Hi, my name is JoAnne. I'm a search angel out of Tucson, Arizona. Is this Marcie Keithley-Roth? And did you place your daughter up for adoption in November 1978?"

Instantly skeptical, but unable to deny she had the right date, I said, "I'm sorry, who did you say you were?"

"I'm what they call a search angel. I help find birth families so they can reconnect. You posted a message on my website this morning and I loved your story. I was working on another case, but when you said you are now married to your child's birthfather and you are looking together, it made your story so compelling. I had to drop everything and see if I could find some answers."

Believing I'd accidentally put my phone numbers into the hands of a scam artist, I lit into her. "Listen, I am Marcie Keithley-Roth, and I did surrender my daughter in November 1978, but I've been looking for months. If you're hoping to make money off of me, I've got news for you, I'm not giving you my credit card information."

The woman cut me off before I could continue my rant. "Marcie, listen to me very carefully. This is not a joke. I found your daughter. Believe me, it's her. I know, because I spoke with her, as well as her adoptive mother."

My hands began to tremble from the adrenaline pumping through my heart. Could it really be true? "How do you know it's her—for sure?"

"Your daughter was a breech birth, correct?"

That little piece of additional information catapulted me into conviction. I hadn't mentioned details of Jesse's birth when posting my story on any of the websites I visited. I dropped the phone and screamed for Roger. Hardly anyone knew I'd delivered breech. It had to be her. This woman had found my Jesse.

JoAnne gave me the number to my daughter's home. She said Jesse, now known as Kara, was anxiously awaiting my phone call. Through near hysterical sobs, I thanked our search angel, then hung up the phone. We had a different call to make.

Supernatural Orchestration

In my office, Roger stood so close I could feel the tremors in his body. On speaker phone, I anxiously dialed the number JoAnne had given me. A precious voice answered within two rings.

"Kara? This is Marcie." I said.

"Mama? Is this you? Is this really you? I knew you'd find me! Oh, my God, I knew it!" she sobbed.

"Yes, it's me honey," I replied, surprised that she called me Mama and that I so easily called her honey. "It's your mother. And I have a surprise for you, too. Your father's here with me."

Roger leaned down and spoke directly into the phone, "Hi baby." His emotions made his voice crack.

For the next few hours, we all talked. Questions and answers flew back and forth, along with three sets of tears. Jesse did not want to get off the phone. We agreed that we needed to meet as soon as possible, so Roger and I offered her a plane ticket. She would fly up from Sarasota, Florida to our home in Southern Indiana. We set the date for the following week.

When we finally hung up four hours later, I sat back, emotionally drained. Though some of the information our daughter had shared was hard to hear and accept, one thing was clear. Our call had come at just the right time. Her adoptive mother, Sandy, whom Jesse lived with, had just been diagnosed with terminal cancer. She was not expected to live over a year and Jesse's adopted father had already passed away. If we hadn't found each other, Kara/Jesse and her children would have been homeless. It was as if everything had been the result of supernatural orchestration.

It's a Girl

After weeks of anticipation, I woke up early on the day of my daughter's scheduled arrival. I felt both thrilled and frustrated. One of the most exciting days of my life had fallen on the date of our monthly managers' meeting at work. We were expected to be seated and ready to begin at 8:00 a.m. sharp. Attendance was mandatory—if you were dying you might get a pass.

For the last seventeen years, I looked forward to this time spent with my co-workers sharing our sales successes for the month, reviewing our profit and loss statements, discussing employee issues, and setting goals for the next month. But today was different. Today was the day I would finally hold my daughter in my arms again—only now, she was a grown woman.

Although she was not scheduled to arrive until 1:00 p.m., I had requested a personal day. Our meetings were held in downtown Louisville, and attendance would require a crazy amount of driving for me. I'd have to cross the bridge once for my meeting, then drive back to get Roger, and then cross the bridge once more to go to the airport. I was already nervous and wanted more time to get everything prepared at home for her visit.

Roger and I had purchased a banner that read *It's a Girl,* and we also ordered a birthday cake that said *Welcome Home, Jesse.* I had borrowed a playpen and highchair for Jesse's two-year-old daughter, our granddaughter, Alyssa. Roger and I wanted everything to be perfect.

The day before, we still weren't finished preparing the guest room for them to sleep in, so the last thing on my mind was attending a work meeting. I wasn't dying, but I thought I had a great excuse for requesting a day off. I was wrong. My regional manager had a different thought process.

Sabotage

When I told my manager I'd be absent, he said, "Why can't you attend our meeting tomorrow, Marcie?" Chuck already knew the answer, but he pushed anyway. "You don't have to be there until 1:00, right?"

I stared back at him, my brow cocked, and my jaw clenched. *Do you not get it? This is my daughter. The daughter I did not know. I'm not playing hooky—this is important!*

I felt utterly sabotaged.

For the last seventeen years, I had given my employer my all. As one of the bank's top performers, I had attended every meeting, every class, and even scheduled my vacations so I could have perfect attendance for any required meetings. I worked evenings and weekends to ensure I obtained my sales goals. After all of this time and dedication, this was what I got for asking to be excused from one meeting.

Insulted by his lack of compassion, but not wanting to let anything ruin my excitement, I decided the effort was not worth a fight. "No problem, Chuck," I lied. "No problem at all. I'll be there."

On the day of Jesse's arrival, though it took a toll on my body, mind, and spirit, I hauled myself back and forth across the bridge to make the meeting, get Roger, and finally head to the airport. In the car, Roger and I sat in silence, each consumed with our own thoughts.

After twenty-nine years, I felt like a long-distance runner who was finally nearing the finish line. My prize awaited me. In a few short hours, our daughter would be in my arms. I would find the long-awaited closure I'd hungered for over the past three decades. Just a little bit longer, and I could run through the banner and pump my tired arms in the air.

I imagined cheering crowds and ecstatic embraces. Instead of a trophy and ribbon, I'd receive peace and forgiveness as my reward for perseverance. My running days were over. I punched the accelerator on the car—my long, sought-after answers were within reach. I was ready to claim my redemption. But unbeknownst to me, something sinister had slithered into my imaginary stadium.

I didn't see it at first, absorbed as I was with my visions for the coming reunion. Coiled like a female rattlesnake waiting patiently to strike on a hot day—she was ready—only this serpent didn't warn. She waited noiselessly for my arrival, ready to reach out and infect me with her venom.

I wouldn't notice her subtle sting at first, but with time, it would weaken me, bring me to my knees, and fill my soul with poison. And I wasn't her only target. She would claim victims besides myself. Her name?

Adoption.

Sometimes, it feels as if life itself is bent on triggering us or sabotaging our desires for happiness and peace. It isn't easy to maintain a steady resolve when life gets messy and the contents of our shoeboxes are beginning to spill out. But perseverance is a key to greater freedom—even when the messiness reveals more shock inside the shoebox.

UNPACKING YOUR SHOEBOX

1. At any time in your life, has another person sabotaged your plans, desires, or dreams? _____

   _____

   _____

   _____

   _____

2. Have you ever seen events align in such a way you almost couldn't deny a divine intervention? _____

   _____

   _____

   _____

   _____

The Shoebox Sherpa's Points to Ponder

- If chronic anxiety, depression, sleeplessness, panic attacks, or any other symptoms of emotional trauma are present, seek the support of a professional therapist, counselor, psychologist, or psychiatrist. It's not the weak who seek help, but the strong.

- Pay attention to your triggers. Look for patterns in the things that upset you. When you identify your triggers, you can reduce the power they hold over your life.

- When you are afraid of taking a first step, breathe deep, and remind yourself that the start is often the hardest part of any healing process.

- Refuse to let anything or anyone get between you and your emotional freedom. Remember, you only get one shot to make the most of the life you've been given.

CHAPTER TWELVE

MESSY BOTTOMS

Hitting rock bottom isn't necessarily a one-and-done event. Some of us seem destined to bounce off of messy bottoms again and again. Have you ever felt like you were on an emotional trampoline you couldn't get off of?

I took a hard bounce when Jesse first came to stay with Roger and me.

The three of us experienced a euphoric time where reunification seemed to solve the problems of our fragmented-by-adoption family. But an unexpected transformation began the first time Jesse spent the night at our home.

As Jesse lay her head on my lap, she looked up and stroked my face. I glanced at my handsome husband, the father of my child who sat beside us, and felt a contrast of utter joy and sadness. I thought of Jesse not as a young woman of twenty-nine, but as an infant. I thought of Roger and myself as the young kids who'd conceived her. The room became crowded as the younger versions of all three of us appeared in my mind.

The full impact of all the minutes, hours, days, weeks, and years—lost and unrecoverable—struck me. Later that night, I cried myself to sleep. And Jesse hadn't told me the whole truth about her adoption yet.

My daughter's childhood did not turn out as Dr. Stanley and his nurse had so attractively painted it. I now know this happens a lot more often than most people realize. In fact, like many other stories told by people I've personally met, Jesse experienced the opposite of picture perfect. She endured chronic child neglect, abuse, and was essentially uneducated.

I can only imagine the level of chaos that went on in the household Jesse was raised in, based on her descriptions as well as documentation we've uncovered. It surprised me to find out the woman who raised my daughter had basically given up on her life and Jesse's, after her husband left her for another woman. My daughter was only three years old. Afterward, Jesse's adoptive father had little to do with her. Upon their respective passings, neither adoptive parent left any provision for Kara/Jessica in their wills.

When she entered her teens, Jesse discovered drug and alcohol abuse as methods for covering her emotional pain. She also sought acceptance and love in many unsavory ways.

Intimate Strangers

Several weeks after our first meeting, Jesse and her three children moved in with Roger and me. Emotionally, we were all in unknown territory, reacting with our hearts, filled with longing, guilt, regret, and remorse. There was no logic in any of it.

My family and friends thought I had lost my mind. Maybe I had. How do you piece your family together after thirty years? Where's the rulebook on that? Jessica was our biological daughter, but she was also a stranger. An intimate stranger.

Roger had already made huge alterations. New marriage, new state, recently retired, step-daughter, step-grandchildren, and now his blood daughter and three more granddaughters were part of his life. It was a lot for him to take in, and for me as well.

Through all of this, I learned I was much stronger than my new husband. Past experience and our present union made me think I could take on the world. I had built a successful career and was not one to shy away from challenges or difficult situations. I naturally looked for ways to make things happen. I was hell-bent on making my family whole—whatever the cost. I had no idea the high price I would pay.

Jesse was severely damaged, physically and emotionally, when she arrived. By twenty-nine years old, she had delivered five children and placed two for adoption, one at birth and one at the age of three. Jesse had dropped out of high school at sixteen and was pregnant by seventeen. Abused and neglected as a small child, she began to "huff" at twelve and began using drugs, alcohol, and sex to fill the brokenness. Her speech and understanding were limited—I needed to speak to her using simple language skills to ensure she understood. It seemed as if her intellect was frozen as a teenager.

I was brokenhearted to learn that like myself, she suffered from epileptic seizures. Many times, she made attempts to get her health information from the state of Pennsylvania but was denied due to her closed birth records.

At one point, I asked Sandy, Jesse's adoptive mother, if she received the extensive medical forms I filled out, so my daughter could have access to her health records. Sandy's reply was simply, "No. We got the baby and were told she was healthy."

I was livid. What was the point of completing medical history forms and disclosing my childhood meningitis and epilepsy if Dr. Stanley had no intention of giving the forms to the adoptive family? Why was Jessica denied access to her files when she was an adult?

"Mom, I tried to find you for years," Jesse said. "They told me unless you gave permission, I couldn't get my medical file or anything about my adoption. But how could I get permission if I didn't know who you were? They said I could find out for $250.00, but I had no money."

Her words filled my soul with sadness and regret. And it got worse.

Lacking knowledge about her medical history, plus the drug and alcohol abuse starting at such a young age, Jessica suffered a stroke at age twenty-two. She was wheelchair bound and unable to walk for several months. It was only after she had the stroke that Sandy told her my name. Jesse's adoptive mother had known my identity the entire time but refused to give it to Jesse for fear she would find me.

I knew nothing about my daughter's adoptive family, but they had my info. So much for birthmother confidentiality, right?

I learned Jessica's three remaining children also suffered. Her sordid choice of men presented a danger to her as well as her children. It also led to our granddaughters being in and out of foster homes. All three were sexually abused. My head spun and my heart raced at this awful news.

This was adoption? This was Jesse's better world? What had I done?

In reality, I knew it wasn't my fault, but I still felt 100% responsible for how Jesse had turned out. Perhaps the result would have been the same if I had raised her, but one thing I felt certain of, my first granddaughter would not be lost in the adoption funnel today.

I struggled to comprehend the truth. How could God answer my prayer of finding Jessica, only to discover my daughter's life was damaged? I was angry and wanted answers.

Why did these people even adopt? How did they slip through the system? The adoption that was marketed to me in 1977 was nothing like I was promised.

And then it hit me. Adoption was not a guarantee of a better life. My daughter just had a different life. Her parents were subject to all the things that could happen to any of us. Divorce, financial disaster, illness, alcoholism, failed businesses, even death. At the time, adoption seemed the better decision, but I made that fatal choice uniformed about the realities of real-life adoption.

If I had a looking glass into the future, I would have seen that I could have raised Jesse if I had just had a little support and encouragement. I wish I'd known!

Roger and I, along with my daughter Michele, did everything we could think of to help Jessica. My husband took her to register her daughters in school, we bought her a van, and our house was large enough to accommodate all of them. Michele babysat for her sister on the weekends while Jesse worked, and tried to get to know her better.

We took Jessica to our physician, as well as a counselor, and all of us went into therapy.

But Jesse's choices of shady men and her uncontrollable actions continued. After several months of receiving calls from men in prison, and dealing with Jesse's other consequences, we were emotionally spent. We feared setting boundaries and losing her all over again, but finally, it all became too much. We sat her down and made our expectations clear. After only eight months, our daughter moved out and the dance began.

Over the next decade, our daughter would move in out of our home, dragging the kids from Florida to Indiana, multiple times. By the third episode, we began to realize this was her life. It would never change. Jesse refused to stay on her meds, discontinued her therapy, and went on with her chosen lifestyle, including drug use.

By 2014, we became estranged, with only a monthly phone call keeping us connected. Finally, in August 2016, she called and told me she was homeless and asked for a bus ticket from Florida. By this time, Jesse's girls were separated from one another. Roger and I had kept the youngest child twice before, and Jesse was ready to send her back to us again. Our oldest granddaughter had been with us since 2014 and was doing well. Jesse's middle daughter moved to Pennsylvania with her father.

In 2016, we gave Jesse a final chance to come home and make her life and her family work. She landed a good job at a distribution center, rented a house, bought her own car and appeared to show significant signs of improvement. However, when Christmas Eve arrived, everything changed again.

She was a no-show.

I loved my daughter and would never turn my back on her, but I decided to turn myself away from her problems and her continued poor choices. Within two years, she was on drugs and homeless again. We took the youngest again, only this time I obtained legal guardianship of her.

As long as she was on drugs and associated with other drug users and felons, I wanted no part of it. Our relationship once again moved to only phone calls and text messages. It was obvious to me by now that there would be no happy ending for us, we were no fairy-tale family. We were all broken and there was no fixing us. We decided to worry most about our granddaughters, at least maybe we could help save them.

The compilation of all of this made me fully grasp the ramifications of Jesse's adoption and how the loss of her original family had impacted her starting in infancy. She was compelled to self-destruction. The emotional damage ran so deep, all of our efforts had failed.

Gone

One day, after Jesse had packed up her entire room once again and was already on a bus headed back to Florida, I stared at the bare room she'd occupied. It looked like she'd taken everything except the bedding we'd bought her. The sheets and pillows were rumpled and wadded up with the comforter. Then, I glanced toward the nightstand, and noticed she'd left one more key item behind.

I curled up on her unmade bed and clutched the music box to my chest. I opened it, and "Amazing Grace" tinkled into the room. My mom had given it to her, a special gift from a grandmother who'd spent decades missing her granddaughter and praying for her.

I brooded. *Why didn't she take it with her? It's so tiny it could have fit in her purse or suitcase. Why would she purposely leave it behind?*

Knowing Jesse could inconsiderately discard my mother's carefully chosen gift hurt me deeply. A child's soft cries interrupted my concerns for my mother's feelings. *Amber.* My granddaughter needed me.

I forced myself out of Jesse's bed and walked toward the sound of Amber's anguish in the next bedroom. I fully understood my granddaughter's pain. *How could Jesse do this to her child? I was five when Mommy left me.*

One day my mommy was with us, the next she was gone. One day I had long beautiful hair, the next I had a short-cropped bob. This was my five-year-old truth. That first year was covered with deep sorrow, overshadowed by loss, while periodic "happy" family times disguised an inner longing for what I missed.

Though I felt the emotional impact of Mommy's sudden departure, I was too young to understand what really happened. Judy stepped in immediately, playing the surrogate mother role. She took the un-asked-for responsibility seriously. But at least one of her attempts brought the whole family laughter. Sometimes, you need a little humor to break up the heaviness.

Just Wonderful

Judy was determined to master meals, so she made an attempt at Aunt Helen's homemade chili. Instead of the scrumptious, hot meal she envisioned, Judy managed to make a pot of burned meat and beans. Mortified, Sissy put the pan in the middle of the table, then slumped in the vinyl chair that matched our green, enamel table. She sat opposite Daddy—in Mommy's seat.

Daddy, determined to encourage her brave attempt, tried to cheer her up. "Dude, this is so good," he said. Dude was Daddy's nickname for Judy.

Confused, I innocently said, "But Daddy, it tastes awful!"

Lifting his eyebrows, he offered me a knowing nod. "Now honey, it's wonderful," he lied.

Turning his attention to my brother, Daddy said, "Isn't that right, Butch? Your sister's chili is just wonderful."

Just by looking at my brother, I knew he was struggling. His face wore an unusual shade of green. Butchie looked like he might puke any minute. But taking Daddy's lead, he just smiled and nodded. Then he washed the repulsive concoction down with a huge gulp of milk.

For years after, we turned to this story as a way of coping with one of the hardest periods of our lives—focusing on the laughter. Holding my granddaughter while she mourned her mother's presence, I hoped we could find something to provide Amber with the kind of laughter that had helped me deal with my immense pain. We were going to need any assistance we could get.

Alone Again

As the weight of our reality with Jesse got heavier, Roger and I began to distance ourselves from other people and each other—though we didn't see it while it was happening. The brokenness of my whole life started haunting me in the form of flashbacks and reflections from my childhood. Jesse's meltdown had triggered a cascade I could not shut off. I too, felt alone again.

My concerns about Jesse and her kids became an obsession. When things escalated to the point I could hardly get out of bed, I took a leave of absence from the bank. Every time I tried to figure things out, it seemed I stepped on an emotional landmine that blew up in my face. I hit rock bottom so many times, it didn't even surprise me anymore. I couldn't imagine things getting any worse. In actuality though, something unimaginable was coming, and it would throw me into the blackest pit I'd ever known.

A Little Hope

I began to ignore my family, friends, career, health, finances, and my marriage. It cost me my job as I practically withdrew from everyday living. Roger was in a similar place. What I had once seen as our fairy-tale love reunion, was unraveling before my eyes, and I was helpless to stop it. I couldn't understand how something that felt so right could go so wrong.

Facing the devastation of my life, I considered suicide. Everything was gone: my career, the daughter I couldn't save, and my fantasy of a marriage. But thankfully, I'm an optimist at heart—and for good reason. That characteristic along with good therapy, helped me recover from the depths of depression and anxiety. A little hope and good news didn't hurt either.

At the beginning of 2017, Jesse finally proved to us she had changed her life. She rented her own home, bought a car, worked at a big distribution plant, and wanted to leave her prior life behind. One day, she astonished us with how far she was willing to go to return to our family.

Jesse asked Roger and I to meet with her. "I want to change my name to the one you gave me when I was born. I want to legally be Jessica," she said.

Roger and I squeezed hands and smiled at each other. I turned back to Jesse and said, "Are you sure? This is a permanent decision."

"It's who I really am," Jesse reasoned. "I want to live my life as the real me."

How could we disagree? Besides, her father and I were thrilled.

That year, for Jesse's birthday, we paid for an attorney who helped legally change Jesse's name back. But Roger had an additional surprise for our daughter.

He suggested we take it a step further to legally adopt her, terminating Jesse's infant adoption after I was pressured into surrendering her. We had no idea our desire to make things right would garner so much attention.

The Associated Press picked up our story from a local Indianapolis report, which led to national and international attention. To date, our story has been front page news on *USA Today*, *The Washington Times*, *London Today*, *The Wall Street Journal*, and others. We've even appeared on *Daily Mail TV*. But our story didn't end with media reels.

Coincidences

There is no such thing as a perfectly happy ending, but Roger and I have learned to accept and love our daughter for who she is. I hear from her daily, and I am grateful for our connection. I've been especially fascinated to learn how much our lives paralleled before we reunited. You will never convince me that coincidences don't exist.

Though raised in completely different cities, my oldest daughter,

Michele, and Jesse, were both baptized in the same church. Raised as Kara, Jesse named her two baby dolls, Jessica and Michele. When I went on vacation to visit friends in 2006, my daughter was five minutes away and I had no idea. And Jesse's youngest daughter, Amber, looks just like Roger, displaying her Pop Pop's bright, blue eyes.

Life has a way of delivering both good and bad in successive cycles, sending many of us to very messy rock bottoms. When Jesse's adoptive mother succumbed to her cancer, it was only the first of many other challenges our daughter had to overcome. And with each pit she had to crawl out of, I was affected as well. Yet, crawl we did, even when darker days came. More disclosures would reveal that I wasn't the only one who kept a secret box.

You think you know people, and you believe you have an understanding about the events of their lives, but sometimes, you find out you are wrong about a few things. Coincidences can come in boxes, too.

UNPACKING YOUR SHOEBOX

1. When did you work really hard at something, only to have it blow up in your face?_____

_____

_____

_____

_____

2. Have you ever experienced clinical depression or debilitating anxiety? Did you know a diagnosis of trauma-related PTSD is not always related to military service? _____

_____

_____

_____

_____

The Shoebox Sherpa's Points to Ponder

- Allow yourself to shed tears if you need to—tears are an integral part of the healing process.

- If you don't know how to create and protect healthy boundaries, make it your mission to learn. There are many resources: experts you can talk with, books, audio and visual aids, conferences, seminars, and trainings.

- If you are prescribed medicine from a professional, make sure you take your meds.

- When your gut tells you that something is off, don't ignore your feelings. Begin to investigate, analyze, and research until you determine what is bothering you.

CHAPTER THIRTEEN

FAMILY BOXES

Fortitude is a trait most of us desire. But who wants to experience the kind of events necessary to instill that growth in us? Yet for some of us, the contents we conceal in our boxes symbolize what has made us stronger, though we falsely see these items as representative of our weakness.

The shoebox effect may start out as a way to try and hide, whether forced to by circumstances, or as a result of inner resolve. When we deal with what we stuff inside our boxes, we transform. Resilience, courage, tenacity, grit, and perseverance begin to define us, versus guilt, embarrassment, humiliation, remorse, and shame. Healthy characteristics that develop through discomfort and pain actually equip us to better deal with any future unexpected and unwanted events.

When I buried my box, those years as a secret-keeper kept me down. But when I revealed the truth about my daughter, I began to feel set free—I rose from the ashes of my past. And I would need that fortitude, resilience, courage, tenacity, grit, and perseverance, because I was about to lose one of the most important people in my life forever—while I discovered a big secret she'd hidden in her own box.

Judy's eyesight began getting poor, and she decided to retire and live with her daughter and grandchildren in Pennsylvania. In reality, my sister, was extremely ill. But we didn't find this out until after she died.

Judy had only lived with her daughter for six months when she was hospitalized. My mom and I wanted so much to go see her, but we weren't in a position to make the trip.

Besides, Jute assured us, "I'm fine. There's no need to bother."

Days later, she suddenly slipped into a coma. I was crushed.

Judy and I had always had a special bond. My earliest memories were of my "Sissy."

Since our parents' divorce when I was five, my big sister had become everything I identified with as security. Only thirteen herself when our parents split, Judy, the oldest among us siblings, became my anchor. While Daddy, a foreman at a chemical plant, worked his swing shift to provide for us, Judy assumed the role of mother.

Until my step-mother Marge entered the picture, during the school year, Jute woke us each morning, fixed breakfast, walked us to the bus stop, then went to school herself. When we arrived home in the afternoons, Judy's "mommy" duties resumed. Each evening, Sissy prepared dinners, washed laundry, and made sure chores and homework were done. She oversaw baths, pajamas, teeth brushing, and helped us lay out our clothes for the next day.

It was my Sissy who comforted me when my little five-year-old heart ached for Mommy. How could the woman who'd curled up in the bed with me, held me close, stroked my face, and distracted me with our very own made up story, *Johnny and the Runaway Bed*, be gone? How could Judy be in a coma?

Suffering

My sister's birthday fell on a Saturday, so Mom, my brother Butch, and myself crowded around the telephone to call our niece and check on Judy. Mary Beth was giving us the solemn update, when Butch said, "Sh, listen.

We huddled closer toward the phone. At first, all we could hear was a muffled gurgle. Seconds later, the sound transformed into a strained rasp. Mommy grabbed the phone and shouted, "Judy. Judy, it's Mama, I'm here. I love you!"

We could hear Judy take a heavy breath. Then in a very slow and measured response, graveled as her voice was, my sister said, "I. Love. You. Mama."

Mommy's emotions were written in the pink tinge on her cheeks and the tears flowing to her chin. She handed the phone to me.

"It's me. It's your sissy. I love you, Jute," I said.

The deep breaths coming through the receiver let us know how much effort my sister was exerting. But it paid off. The last words my sister spoke came in that precious moment when she drew out the words, "I. Love. You. Sissy." Then we heard a rustling sound.

My niece came back on. "I'm sorry. She's getting restless. I've got to go." Then the line went dead.

Our little family sat still and silent. Numb. So happy Judy had been able to speak—so sad because we felt what was coming. In five days, my sister would take her last breath.

I hated watching my parents suffer, Daddy was nearing ninety years old and Mommy was eighty-five. When my brother broke the news to our father, he didn't cry, but kept rubbing his head as if it were a dream he could wake himself up from.

"My poor Dude," he said sadly. "Here I sit in a wheelchair and my beautiful daughter is gone." He shook his head.

We eventually found out that Judy had lung cancer, from years of chain-smoking. Though we can't verify it, we believe she knew and did not want Mom to see her pass, but we'll never be able to confirm it. Her sudden departure left all of us in shock and caused each of us to process her passing in our own way.

Honoring Judy

When I was asked to give Judy's eulogy, I not only honored my sister's life, but found a way to bring her personality into it. My strong-willed, fiercely loving sister would have wanted it that way.

I shuffled my papers nervously on the podium. "Judy left us so quickly, and we're all still trying to wrap our minds around it," I said.

"There was no time for goodbyes. How do you sum up a joyous, unforgettable life in ten minutes? You remember their highlights and talk about what you learned from knowing them. Judy taught me so much.

"My big sister never stopped telling me what to do, right up until the very end. We didn't always agree, and sometimes we'd go without speaking for weeks, but Judy never let our disagreements go on too long.

"The phone would ring, and when I answered, I'd hear her voice saying, 'Pack a bag and come spend the night with me, Mace.' I loved snuggling on the couch with my Sissy, eating Haagen Dazs and watching 48 Hour mysteries. Time after time, she said the same thing with a wink, 'Isn't this a great Saturday night date? Who needs a man when you've got your sister and Haagen Dazs?'

"I learned to appreciate the little things and ordinary moments, because of Judy.

"My sister's contagious laugh and determination to find humor in everything made her fun to be around. Don't we all want to be around someone who makes life more enjoyable instead of adding to our misery? I've always wanted to be more like her in that way.

"A constant reader, Judy was quick-witted, sharp, and had excellent recall. She was an expert at trivia and loved the Jeopardy game show. All of this made her a great communicator and interesting conversationalist. For years, family members, including myself, begged her to audition for the show, but she refused. For all of her sassy boldness and flare for the dramatic, my sister sometimes lacked confidence. And that was the paradox about my sister. For all her bravado and the times she took charge, she could also be insecure and almost childlike. But Judy found a way to make those positive traits.

"Instead of looking inward at herself, my sister looked to the needs of others, often ignoring her own to meet them. She perfected sacrificial giving. I, too, want to serve people and make a difference the way Judy did.

"Throughout her career, Judy spent decades in the housing and leasing business. She worked at various apartment complexes, leasing apartments, and worked for one builder in Indianapolis for many years. She dabbled in home mortgages for a while, even working with me for a time. All of this experience finally led her to the doors of Capital Court. What started out as just another leasing job turned into something that became her calling. And some might say, her ministry.

"Reaching a certain age herself, Judy felt the plight of her older tenants. She made herself available to them 24/7. If someone fell in the middle of the night and pulled the cord, Judy was there to help. If one of her tenants died, it was Jute that consoled their families. They became her extended family and she theirs. I see some of them here with us today. We should all aspire to touch lives in positive ways like Judy did.

"My sister was an avid card sender. Sometimes she would send you two—one funny, one serious. She chose her cards carefully, making sure the message was always heartfelt and genuine. And she sent them the good old-fashioned way, buying a stamp and mailing them. She loved giving cards.

"It is in this spirit that I wonder, if Judy was with us, if she could send a final card or letter to us, what would it say? Let's imagine Judy's sent us a personal note, think of it as a 'Hallmark from Heaven,' written with her personality. This is what I think she would tell us.

Dear Family and Friends:

I guess by now you've already heard about the celebration going on in heaven right now. Can you believe it? And it's all for me! You cannot possibly imagine the magnificence of being in the presence of God. It's just like the Bible says and more.

Since I didn't get a chance to say good-bye to most of you, I wanted to take a moment to tell you some things you already know, but probably need to hear.

I left the earthly world behind me with no regret. My

life there was simply amazing. For you see, I was one of the lucky ones.

In my sixty-seven years, I was able to experience love. I saw the sun set in California. I watched my daughter take her first breath, heard my grandson's first cries, and lived to see my great-granddaughter. I swam in the ocean and slept under the stars. I got to be a wife and mother. How remarkable is that?

I wanted to be with you all, especially my daughter, Mary Beth, and her boys, but my time was up. Please remember to pray for them in the coming days and months. All of you, stay in touch with one another.

I'll bet you didn't know this about me, but I was rich. I got to be someone's daughter. And I wasn't blessed with just two parents, I got four. Two who gave me life, and two who shared my life.

Thank you, Mom, for not only giving me life on earth, but for showing me how to obtain the eternal one. You were and always will be my best friend.

Daddy, I was always so proud of the sacrifice you made as a young marine, fighting overseas. I never grew tired of hearing your stories. I hope I did you proud by my work at Capital Court, sending packages and letters to our soldiers.

To my brother Butch. You are in charge now. Our parents will need you now more than ever. Continue to remain close and support them with your love and kindness.

To my little sisters, Marcie and Lorraine. The bond between us can never be broken, not even in death. Make special time for yourselves and don't let life get in the way of your time together. Remember to have your annual sister's day and when you do, think of me, as I will be right there with you.

I could go on and on, so many people to mention, and so many things I still want to say. But God has a schedule up here and it's time to go. Take heart in knowing I loved you all and will be waiting for you on the other side. Don't be sad. Celebrate my life. For saying goodbye is another way of saying, I remember. And I do.

This is my last Hallmark from Heaven.

All my love, Jute

P.S. I finally quit smoking, LOL."

A harmony of sniffles filled the room. After reading *Judy's Hallmark from Heaven*, I shared *Five Things We Love About Judy*, given to me by her residents.

1. She had a beautiful smile for us each day.
2. She cared for the less fortunate.
3. She was funny and bright.
4. She put others before herself, even when things got tough.
5. Working with us was more than just a job to her. She loved us.

Chuckles flitted around the room as much as tears, while people imagined what their personal "Hallmark from Heaven" from Judy might say, and thought about what they loved about my sister. Scanning their faces and seeing a hint of a smile on both of them, the thought seemed to give my parents a little peace.

I added my concluding remarks. "I feel my sister's presence everywhere, from the Iris's she planted in the front of the Capital Court building, to the stacks of items packed in the corner to send to our troops overseas, to the people sitting in this room. Judy left her print on everyone she came in contact with."

We closed the service with the Beatles singing, "Hey, Jude," as a spoof on Judy's nickname, Jute.

Goodbye for Now

When I walked outside after the service, I looked up into the sky. Judy and I had made a promise to each other that whoever died first would send the other one a sign that we had reached Heaven and were okay. I drove myself crazy waiting for the white dove we agreed on as our symbol to show up and give me the sign. It didn't happen the day we buried her.

Eight months after Jute died, my stepmother also died. During my last months with Marge, I would come and stay with her and Daddy every Friday. I made dinner, did Marge's nails, and we would girl-talk. She knew she didn't have long to live and wanted to spend as much time as possible with all of us. She and my mom even exchanged letters—Mommy thanked Marge for being so good to us.

On one of those visits, Marge and I reflected on memories of our home on Clifton Avenue. We had camped, celebrated holidays, hosted Girl Scouts, worked through dreaded math problems, and of course, explored shorthand there. Tough times and sad times, we faced them all. I told Marge how much I loved her and what a difference she had made in my life.

My younger sister Lorrie and I knew the end was getting closer, so we decided to have a slumber party. We chose a Friday night for both of us to stay with her (I usually gave Lorrie a break on Fridays). My Lexus was packed and ready to go. I headed to work for a couple of hours and was just getting ready to start the forty-five-minute trip for our slumber party, when Lorrie called me on my cell. "She's gone. Mama's gone."

Shaken, I sped toward Daddy and Marge's house. When I arrived, other family members were filtering in. Butch was the last one to join us. I watched my brother kneel beside Marge's bed, hold her hand, and softly thank her for all the times she was there for him. "I wouldn't have made it without you. You saved me."

In fact, Marge saved all of us. In less than a year, I gave my second eulogy. For Marge, I titled it, *A Walk Through the Garden of My Life.*

The day we laid my stepmother to rest was beautiful in every way. The sun shone from bright skies and fluffy clouds. She loved her garden, and the flowers surrounding Marge's casket were of many varieties she loved. It was as if God kissed his own handiwork and opened Heaven's gate to give us all a tiny glimpse of what Marge was now enjoying.

I pulled into my driveway a few hours later, exhausted and sad, but thankful this beautiful woman had entered my world and changed the course of my life. I shut my car door and looked up. And there, on top of my house, looking regal and strong, sat a beautiful white dove. Judy was honoring Marge, too.

Just ten months after my beloved stepmother passed, Daddy died, followed by my kind-hearted stepfather, and lastly, Aunt Helen at the age of 97. Within five years, I lost five of the most stable people in my life. I had to say, "Goodbye, for now," too many times.

Daddy was given full military honors and a final salute from the Indiana Association of Volunteer Fire Fighters. I was proud of my father, what he gave to our country, and his community. For most of my life, he was a harsh parent, but the last several months prior to his passing changed his personality. He expressed kindness toward his children. And finally, I heard those words I had longed for my entire life. Daddy said, "I love you."

I'm not sure how I made it through that time of intense mourning, but I do know the back-to-back losses caused me to delay dealing with many things. This is why it was several years after Judy's death, before I gathered the gumption to clean out my garage, which led to the discovery of Judy's box.

A Serious Talk

The Saturday afternoon heat felt oppressive, but I was determined to organize every corner. I'd worked for hours when I stumbled on a storage tote of Jute's. I'd forgotten she'd left it there when she moved to Pennsylvania. At first, I just stared. I couldn't deal with it. I finally garnered my courage to look through the only possessions I had left from Judy's past.

I took a deep breath and said, "Oh Sissy. Oh, my sweet sissy." Then I pulled the lid off of the burgundy tote.

Inside were photos of Judy's grandchildren, drawings and paintings her daughter and grandson had given her, pictures of some of the properties she'd managed, and old business cards. But separated from the other mementos was a small, plain box. When I opened it and looked inside, I discovered a tiny pair of blue booties, a lock of hair, and a secret letter written in pencil. I read it.

"What?" I said to the empty garage. My shaking hands rattled the edges of the forty-nine-year-old piece of paper.

In shock, I read it again. "I can't believe this," I said out loud, before scanning it one more time to ensure I was really seeing the words I thought I'd read. Then I put everything back inside the little box. I cradled it under my arm as I got into my car. Mommy and I needed to have a serious talk.

Roger was mowing the lawn when I found the box hidden at the bottom of Jute's tote. I was pulling out of the drive when I yelled, "I have to go to Mom's."

He looked at me curiously.

I said breathlessly, "I have to go, I'll call you later." Then I sped away.

While I drove, my mind shifted back to what I'd just read in the letter penned by Judy, dated 1966. How could I not have known?

When I arrived at Mom's house, I knocked on the door, then rushed in without waiting for anyone to answer. In the living room, my stepfather was standing—I hadn't given him time to walk toward the foyer. I gave him a quick hug, then I settled onto the ottoman across from my mother who was seated on the couch.

I held out the box taken from my garage, and tapped the top, where my fingers kept Judy's tattered letter firmly in place, spread out over the lid. "Mommy, do you know about this?" I said.

Mom's eyes were glued to the letter. "I knew this day would come," she said sadly. "I tried to talk to her over the years, but she kept telling me to let it be."

Box of Pain

In 1966, my sister wrote down her feelings of grief, guilt, and the lifetime of pain she knew she would have to carry. A lock of hair, a pair of booties, and this letter hidden in a tiny box told the story of her baby boy, surrendered to adoption. Mom not only knew, but she was with Judy, and had held him before he was taken away.

"I have a box too, for my Jesse," I said. "I was so desperate to escape all the pain I felt after they took my daughter, that I used a shoebox to hide my memories in. I guess I was trying to contain my demon. And now, to find out Jute did the same thing. If only I'd known how much she understood about my futile attempts to bury it so I could survive."

Mom nodded silently.

I continued to pour my soul out. "When my daughter was born, it must have opened up all of Judy's old wounds from the past. I feel so bad for her."

Mom reached out and gently took my hands inside hers. "I'll be right back. Stay put," she said. Then she released me, got up, and left the room.

Less than two minutes later, Mom returned—only she wasn't empty handed. She laid an old shoebox in front of me. "You and Judy are not the only ones who have a box of pain," she said.

I tried to process what she was doing and what she meant, but I felt very confused.

Mom gently laid the box in my lap. My mind was still trying to take it all in as I lifted the lid. Then the revelation of Mom's contents smacked me across the face—I began to weep.

Shoebox Healing

I gingerly fingered the items inside Mom's box: letters I wrote her as a child, one of my drawings, and a poem I wrote titled, "Alone." After moving things around, I saw a small, faded pink piece of tissue paper. My mother had obviously taken special care to lovingly preserve something for safekeeping.

My fingers trembled slightly as I pulled the tissue back, then I gasped. My ponytail lay inside, the one my mother had cut off the day before she left in 1960. I had always associated the cutting of my hair with my mother's leaving. I never could understand why she dressed me up, had my picture taken, then cut my hair and left me the next day.

I looked up from the box and searched my mother's ashen face. "Why, Mommy? Why did you cut my hair off? I never understood why you did that."

I watched as my mom slowly closed her eyes. Based on what she said in response, she must have gone back to that fateful day in her mind. The day she left me behind.

"I knew I wouldn't be there to take care of it anymore, honey." My mom dropped her chin to her chest.

I swallowed hard, then I got up and wrapped my precious mother in a massive hug. After all these years, she had given me the answer to one of my life's most haunting questions. Mommy didn't cut my ponytail off because I'd been bad or because she didn't want me. She'd done it out of love—believing she was doing what was best for me, since she would no longer be there to care for my hair.

Once again, bringing the shoebox out of hiding and facing its contents had not brought about the results we feared. Instead, the truth opened our hearts to begin healing.

Later that night, as I lay in bed absorbing the unforeseen events from the day, I reflected on the impact of three women in the same family with three secret boxes. As close as we were, we never talked about the shoebox effect, and how we'd each used ours to try and survive our excruciating situations. We felt desperate to escape it, so we hid instead of healed.

By knowing the contents of Mommy's box, as well as my own, we were finally able to acknowledge our past and free ourselves from the pain that held us captive for so long. Finally, after many years, my questions were answered. The demons were gone.

I decided to take the foundation of my shoebox healing and build on it. I found a therapist that specializes in helping mothers who have surrendered children to adoption come to a place of peace and acceptance. I also began connecting with other mothers from the adoption community and started a course of self-study on adoption laws. As I listened to what other women shared, I saw common threads in all of our stories.

I learned about the cruelty of the "Baby Scoop Era" where mothers were blindly separated from their babies, who were then given to strangers for a price. I learned the facts about altered birth certificates, buried details, destroyed records, and the denial of vital, lifesaving information for adoptees. So much of the knowledge I gained infuriated me, and I was tempted to lash out, but instead, I chose to channel my anger into adoption reform. Over time, I found deeper fortitude and purpose in sharing information with others. Only one question remained unanswered for me.

Where was Judy's son?

UNPACKING YOUR SHOEBOX

**The Shoebox Sherpa's
Points to Ponder**

- None of us knows how long we have on Earth. Go through your boxes now, separate your mementos and label them for those you want to leave them with, write down your stories, and write letters to tell your loved ones how you feel.

- Have you ever received a sign or symbol that reminded you of someone you love?

- Think back to life-altering moments in your life. What do you assume about those events and the people who were involved? Is there any chance motives, reasons, and intentions were different than what you thought?

- If you have been unfairly treated, had something precious taken from you, or endured unrelenting grief of any kind, look for ways to use what you've learned as a teaching tool. You cannot change what has happened to you, but you can commit to doing something positive with your pain.

1. Have you ever been surprised to find out that a family member and you shared a similar secret? Are there any secrets you'd be ashamed for people to discover after you were gone? What if revealing it now could bring healing to you and others while there's still time?

_____

_____

_____

_____

2. How do you want people to honor you when you die? What would your *Hallmark from Heaven* say? _____

_____

_____

_____

_____

CHAPTER FOURTEEN

HIRAETH HEALING

I believe any woman who has surrendered her child understands the meaning of Hiraeth, even if she's never heard the word or definition. Hiraeth is a Welsh concept, describing a longing for home. Though sources say it cannot be fully translated, it is said to mean missing something or missing home. Hiraeth also alludes to a missing time, era, or a person—including homesickness for what may no longer exist. It is associated with the bittersweet memory of missing something or someone, while being grateful for their existence[4].

I certainly related to this, as I continued to unpack the emotions connected to the discovery of Judy's box, and Mom's as well. Thankfully, my mother was willing to sit down with me and fill in the gaps from the parts of their stories I didn't know.

She said, "Back in the 1960s, though women's rights were being fought for and won, society's overall view of how a woman should act, what her house should look like, how she should behave as a girlfriend or wife, or how she made a living, were much more restrictive than today. But things are changing—though very slowly."

I nodded, signaling Mom to continue.

"The Equal Pay Act of 1963 was signed into law by President Kennedy, improving women's pay scales. The Civil Rights Act of 1964, prohibiting discrimination based on gender, among other important stipulations, increased hiring opportunities for women. And women's

---

4 https://en.wikipedia.org/wiki/Hiraeth

voices started being heard in public forums. But when it came to how a woman's pregnancy was treated, there was little change.

"During this time, also known as the Baby Scoop Era, where an estimated 2 million babies were adopted out in the 1960s[5], Judy got pregnant. She never disclosed who the father was, and he apparently was unwilling to help her."

My spirit felt broken for my sister, as I recalled my own struggles with Roger when I found out I was pregnant with Jesse. I also remembered how strongly Judy reacted to him during that time. No wonder. She was empathizing with me because of what she'd went through.

Mom continued, "Your father divorced me by then, so she and I lived in Indianapolis together, sharing an upstairs apartment. We both worked hard waiting tables, but we barely made enough to pay the rent or feed ourselves. Neither of us had a car or phone."

"I had no idea things were that bad. I'm so sorry, Mommy," I said. I thought about all the assumptions I'd made about the wonderful life Mom and Judy had together, while I was stuck with Daddy and Marge. Now, I better appreciated Marge, and understood why Mommy didn't take me, too.

"You were still young," she said. "Once Judy began to show, the landlord approached me and told me that Judy should place the baby up for adoption."

"What?" I said. "Judy's baby was none of their business."

Mom sighed. "Back then, society shunned unwed mothers. People felt they had the right to speak their mind and heap shame on a mother and child." Mom's eyes welled. "Judy felt the stigma, up close and personally. The landlord wasn't the only one who ostracized her."

"Oh?" I said.

"Judy begged me to help her keep the baby. So as much as I dreaded it, I eventually made a call to your daddy, begging him for help. His response was swift and firm."

---

5 https://en.wikipedia.org/wiki/Baby_Scoop_Era

He said, "I don't want anything to do with this. Keep her away from me while she's pregnant."

Poor, Jute, I thought.

"As her due date grew closer, with no baby items, no family support, no circle of friends to throw baby showers and help out with childcare, no father willing to step up, Judy finally relented to the pressures. She agreed to surrender her child to adoption. Financially, there was just no way she could keep her baby and work. Emotionally, giving up her child was the only way to receive your dad's forgiveness for her sin. So, she signed the papers."

I couldn't believe what I was hearing. How was it possible my sister and I had shared such tragic similarities, and yet, she'd never said a word?

Mom wiped the edge of her eye before concluding. "I was at the hospital when Judy's baby was born—she named him Brian. I got to hold my newborn grandson. I felt like I was letting both him and Judy down. As you know, back then, no one counseled or offered therapy to young, single moms. The attitude was, 'Sign here, and hand us your infant.'"

I held my breath while Mommy's mind seemed to slip into another place and time.

"I touched his tiny fingers and toes and prayed he would go to a good home. I was so scared and worried for your sister and that baby. I begged God, 'If you will just place Brian in a good home with a good family, I promise I won't interfere in his life.'"

I couldn't help thinking how untreated wounds eventually fester and become infected, and how secrets always resurface.

Mom looked resolutely into my eyes. "I've held on to my promise for fifty years, but it's time. Will you help me find him? Will you help me find Brian before I die? He just has to know how wonderful his mother was."

The grief behind those beautiful eyes of my mother was more than I could stand. And I fully understood her heart. I knew that pain all too well. Well-seasoned in the adoption game, I also knew where to start the search for my nephew. I'd learned a lot since I found Jesse.

Finding Chris

Since 2009, I'd advocated for open records in my home state of Indiana and worked with the adoption community nationwide. I'd even testified multiple times as Vice President for H.E.A.R. (Hoosiers for Equal Access to Records) and sat down with then-Governor Mike Pence.

Moms like me usually want to be a part of adoption reform. Many of us were pressured into surrendering our children and silenced when we tried to question what was happening, so we are driven to help other birth parents reclaim their voices. Legislators use the term *birth-mother confidentiality* like it was a part of our relinquishment contract to protect us, which it was not and does not. In fact, few birth parents I've met were given a copy of what they signed—I wasn't.

This birthmother confidentiality term was really used to erase the original identity of the infant and craft a new one with the adoptive family. It was to protect the adoptive family from intrusion from the birthmother. The hope was that by eliminating information access, the child would never learn anything about his/her origins, no matter how much they wanted to know.

On March 4, 2016, Indiana bill, SEA 91, successfully passed, allowing access to records (with restrictions) for all adoptions finalized prior to January 1, 1994. The records would open starting on July 1, 2018. But for those who didn't want to wait until then, like me, there were other potential ways to hunt, though they weren't as easy. I needed to find my nephew as badly as I'd needed to find my daughter.

I registered a Mutual Consent Registration with the State of Indiana Vital Records in Indianapolis first. If my nephew was looking for his birth family, his information would be there. I completed the forms, submitted them, then waited.

After several weeks, a response letter arrived. Needing emotional support, I called my friend, Pam, a close friend and adoptee advocate who co-founded many initiatives alongside me. With Pam on the phone, I tore the envelope open and snatched the letter from inside.

The couple of sentences made my heart fall. My nephew was not registered.

Pam encouraged me to move forward. I took the next step and hired a Confidential Intermediary, or CI. These are court-approved individuals who act on behalf of either an adoptive parent, a birth parent, or an adoptee, in an attempt to make contact.

The fees for a CI range from $200.00 to $1,000.00. They prepare a petition for the court, request adoptee files from the state, including their original birth certificate and the names of the family that adopted the infant. If located, the CI makes the initial call to inform the adoptee that their birth family is looking for them and asks permission for contact. But this is a one-shot call. If the adoptee says no, it's over.

On August 31, 2016, I received a call from the CI who was working on Brian's case. The message was simple. "I found your nephew."

I immediately grabbed my keys, went outside, and jumped in the car.

Crossing Paths

Minutes later, I held Mommy's hands gently in my own. "We found him. We found Brian," I said. "Well, except his birth parents named him Chris. So, we found Brian/Chris," I laughed.

At 6:00 p.m., I called the number provided by the CI for my nephew. We chatted for over an hour—our family bond was instant. Mom was too emotional to get on the phone at first, so she let me handle the onset of the conversation. But when she heard Chris and me laughing and speaking so comfortably together, the anticipation became too much.

Acting as excited as a little kid reaching for their new bike, Mom grabbed at the phone. "I want to talk to him," she said.

After that, I could hardly get the telephone back from her, but I was fine with it. Seeing my mom so happy made my heart swell. And this was only the first of many calls.

Several weeks later, Mommy was reunited with Chris, and I got to meet him for the first time, at his 50th birthday celebration. Mom gave him Judy's Bible, along with a letter she had written him, in case she died before we found him. For the longest time, my mother could not let go of Chris's hand. They sat on the sofa together, drinking coffee one-handed.

Chris's adoption experience was the total opposite of my Jesse's. He was adopted by a loving family and blessed with the security of a stable home and all it had to offer. We were thrilled to discover that he is happily married with three grown children, and even has grandchildren. He still lives in Indianapolis, where he enjoys a healthy, peace-filled, beautiful life.

Several months after we met Chris, Mom and I made the short trip back to Indy to the home of his adoptive mother, so the two women could meet. The Indianapolis Star joined and interviewed all of us. They also made a short video.

Chris described the surreal experience of our two families merging together. In the interview, he said, "It's exciting. It's scary. But at the end it's just love. I mean, it's family."

Through Chris, God gave a little piece of Jute back to us. He has her sense of humor and loving personality. And we found out their paths even crossed before she passed.

There were a few coincidences that brought Chris close to us before we knew him. He got his hair cut in the strip mall where my mom managed a floral shop. He and Judy also worked in the same industry. We also learned that he and my sister were in very close proximity for a bit. As newlyweds, Chris and his wife lived in an apartment complex my sister managed. I only wish Judy would have known it was him, because based on what Mom told me and the contents my sister hid away in her shoebox, she never stopped longing for her son.

Facing My Past

The shoebox effect symbolizes our Hiraeth—a longing for something we miss. It became obvious to me that Chris, Judy's only son, was her Hiraeth. Mom's Hiraeth was me, reflected in the keepsakes she kept in her box, including my ponytail.

In turn, part of my Hiraeth was my Mommy, lost to me when I was five. But on a sultry, Indian Summer day, as I pondered the ache I'd carried in my soul for decades, I realized the depth of my Hiraeth came from more than one source.

To heal, I needed to revisit my past, dig down and unearth what I had spent my entire life trying to avoid, and fully release my emotions. To finally put the lid on the shoebox effect, I had some messages to share.

Through intensive work and therapy, I finally managed to face my past in order to put it behind me and forgive both of my parents for the anxieties they instilled in me at a young age. I've also had to gather my courage and ask others to forgive me. I've found you don't need to fill reams of paper with words to express how you feel—a short, concise, but heart-felt message can offer a depth of meaning. I hope by letting you see messages I've written for my loved ones, it might inspire you to write your own. Healing starts when we rightly use the power of words.

Daddy

Dear Daddy,

I'm so glad you finally asked to see the granddaughter you never knew, even though it didn't happen until three months before you passed. I wish you could have enjoyed the kinds of relationships you had during the last days of your life, when we were all younger. But some people never get that opportunity at all, so I am grateful. I'm also thankful you brought Marge into my life after you and Mommy divorced. It was a hard time, and she helped me so much.

Mommy

Dear Mommy,

I'm so happy God gave you back to me, so we could share this last chapter of your life together. I'm glad you found forty-nine years and seven months of love with Mike, before he passed. He was a wonderful stepfather. And I'm thrilled we are getting to write our mother/daughter devotional together. At 90 years old, you have many stories to tell and much wisdom to impart.

Roger

Dear Roger,

Though we have found we love each other better separated, you will always be connected to my heart. We are bound by the choices of our youth, and I'm glad I have you to share those memories with. For too many years, I blamed losing our daughter on you for hurting and leaving me, but neither one of us were faultless. We were simply trying to figure out how to escape our pasts and lessen life's hurts. Little did we know we were adding to them. We just didn't know. Thank you for your unconditional acceptance and the good relationship we share today. I am grateful we can enjoy our grandchildren together, and especially, that we share our daughter, Jessica.

Michele

Dear Michele,

You are my firstborn—the kept sibling. I am so sorry that in trying to save your sister, I hurt you both. I regret being the "absent" mom while you were growing up. I realize now that my relinquishment of Jesse wasn't just my loss but caused a gap for each of us. I know that kept siblings sometimes suffer from survivor's guilt, and it hurts me to think you might feel bad in any way. If I could take all of your painful emotions away I would— you are wonderful and so very special. I cannot imagine my life without you, and I hope I never find out what it feels like. You are and always have been one of the best things in my life. Thank you for being you.

Jessica

Dear Jesse,

You are now our child legally as well as biologically, as it always should have been. I am so glad you exist and thank God for reuniting us. You've made my life richer, and I know your dad feels the same. None of us are perfect, and we're all still trying to figure out our new normal, but I'm very happy that we are together to work on it as a family. Thank you for being strong, committed, and loving, and especially for not giving up. Your life is a gift, I only wish I could have unwrapped it years earlier.

My Grandchildren

> *My Precious Grandbabies,*
>
> *Each one of you holds a unique and deeply special place inside my soul. We share more than blood, we share spirit. To say I love you is not adequate—I appreciate, enjoy, and admire you. Thank you for lighting up my life and giving it spark. I am grateful for those of you I get to interact with on a regular basis, I miss those of you I cannot see when I want. But I pray for you all. When I call you precious, that is not a word I use lightly, I mean it, you are cherished, treasured, and highly valuable to me.*

Too often, we go through life as intimate strangers with the people we love. We avoid certain topics in fear they might open up a Pandora's Box, so we take an opposing approach. Many of us stuff reminders of those topics inside shoeboxes or other containers, in hopes we can hide the situation away. But this is a mistake.

Through my personal experience, I've learned the biblical passage in John 8:32 is accurate—the truth *does* set us free. Keeping secrets is what holds us captive.

Resolution

In the last several years, because of a simple nudge by my beloved pet who dislodged my long-lost shoebox, I began a journey I never dreamed was possible. By revisiting my past and doing the hard work to heal, I found the true secret to peace and acceptance. I had longed for this since childhood. My quest took me to many people and places, including my sister's grave, but there was still one physical location I needed to revisit—home. Or at least, the place I always associated with it.

In my mind, 1587 Clifton Avenue was filled with family ghosts—this was where I needed to search for the missing pieces of me. When

I pulled up to the curb, I noticed the *For Rent* sign, along with the empty driveway. My pulse palpitated as I got out and approached the house.

Things were different, but my mind brought the missing parts back into clear focus. I recalled the hours Judy and I sat on the front porch, now missing, playing jacks. I could still see the redbud tree near the fence line that bloomed each spring, replaced with heart-shaped leaves in the summer. I looked over my shoulder, to ensure I was still alone, then tried the door knob. To my amazement, it creaked open. I decided it was fate and stepped inside to snoop.

The house looked tiny in comparison to the looming shadows pictured in my mind. I made my way through the living room and walked slowly down the hallway, letting my fingers trail the walls as I relived happy moments from young Marcie's past. I peeked my head in and out of various bedrooms and bathrooms and noted how each had been altered. After circling back to the living room, I realized only one part of the house was still intact—the fireplace—the heart of our home.

I sat on the hearth, and let years of family memories, laughter, and tears flow unhindered. The thoughts came before the sniffles ended. Why was I driven to return here? Why did this little old house on a dead-end street continue to pull me in after all these years? It felt like a full-circle moment—just what was left for me to discover at Clifton Ave.?

Looking at the brick and mortar on the wall next to me, I realized this tiny house was just that—a house. Its contents may have been moved or altered, but its foundation and its heart, the fireplace, still stood strong and regal. This house had survived the toughest of storms, the harshest of weather, and endured many renovations, but it remained standing. Just like me.

The longing for home I felt, this place I yearned to be in, was not a physical location after all, but a place in my heart that was always there, kept alive by both good and bad memories. I had chased money, career, success, and even love, but that child Marcie locked inside my soul, the broken child with the missing ponytail who clutched her Jiminy Cricket, needed to know she was okay. I hugged her tight and assured her I would take care of her.

After experiencing divorce, death, a fall from grace, loss and abandonment, shame and secrets, I had learned something about the true meaning of surrender. If we face our past, do the recovery work, and engage in therapy, but do not forgive, there is no surrender—there is no peace.

It took ten years from the time Dreyfus knocked my shoebox over, before I made it back to Clifton Avenue. A lot had happened, but most importantly, I had relearned the definition of surrender. In my mind, it was no longer a dirty word. I now knew surrender is not defined as giving up, but giving in—giving in to peace, acceptance, and listening to the whispers of your heart. Surrender is pursuing your Hiraeth. It brings you to a place of resolution.

As I got back in my car and smiled through tears of contentment, I could just imagine my sister, Judy, standing on the old porch with her hands on her hips, blue eyes shining, with a huge smile on her face. I wondered what part, if any, she'd had in instigating me to start and stay on this quest.

I looked toward heaven and spoke to the one who helped me come to terms with the shoebox effect. "Good boy, Dreyfus, good boy," I said.

Driving off, I shook my head. It really is true—you can never escape the story of your life, or the pieces of it you try to pack away.

So, let me ask you. What's in *your* shoebox?

UNPACKING YOUR SHOEBOX

1. What is the source of your Hiraeth? Who do you need to write a note or letter to? Who do you need to call? Who or what do you need to remember?

_____

_____

_____

_____

_____

2. Are you possibly part of someone else's Hiraeth? If so, how can you help them reach resolution? _____

_____

_____

_____

_____

The Shoebox Sherpa's Points to Ponder

- Set a goal date, where you commit to sit down and write letters (whether you ever send them or not), to the people who are part of your Hiraeth. Write how you feel/felt, what you wish would have been different, but also share what you are grateful for.

- Forgiveness is a powerful release agent—and the pathway to lasting peace. Consider releasing unresolved bitterness, anger, frustration, or resentment for situations that cannot be changed. Free yourself from chains keeping you captive.

- For any physical location connected to your memories or unresolved grief, if at all possible, go back and revisit it. The sights, sounds, smells, touches, and tastes from the past can stir our spirits like little else, dredging up emotions we need to unearth, so we can finally heal.

- Consider the thoughts, opinions, assumptions, and hurts you are holding onto. Give yourself the gift of full surrender.

EPILOGUE

My volunteer work in the adoption community first began when I discovered the truth about the damage caused by closed records. The heartache of knowing what happened to my daughter and the delay in her search to find me, as well as why she couldn't, stirred my anger. Channeling that pain and frustration, I immediately took our personal story to the media, and found there was great interest.

After our story first went public in October 2009, both from the article on the front page of the Louisville CJ and from the WHAS TV interview, I received numerous emails and phone calls. Adoptees and birthparents alike were seeking help and support.

One 79-year-old woman emailed to say she had just found out by accident that she was adopted through a Catholic Church. She kept repeating how her life was a lie, and she had no idea who she was.

A classmate from school, *a girl that went away,* who I had not seen since 1973, contacted me to tell me she had a baby at age fourteen and never said a word about it to anyone. She was a recovering alcoholic. She told me how brave I was and cried, begging me to release her from the guilt and regret she felt. We made plans to meet for lunch in two weeks, after she had a minor procedure. There were complications and she died in surgery. She has a daughter out there somewhere who will never know her story and that her mom was desperate to find her.

A deputy sheriff stopped by my house one day to look at an automobile I was selling, and after talking for a little bit about my story (he recognized me from the TV interview), he broke down and cried. He told me he was adopted and asked if I could help him.

An older customer of mine came into the bank after my story was featured on the cover of *Southern Indiana Living Magazine*. She confessed she had surrendered her little girl in 1960.

An investment client met with me one day and told me she had terminal cancer. She said she wanted to do some estate planning. I held her hands as she wept in my office and told me she was a mom who had surrendered her child in 1958. She never married, built a small fortune, and wanted help in finding her 'little girl.' Her great desire was to leave all her money to the baby she had never seen.

These are only a handful of the birth stories people have shared with me. This is an emotionally charged and sensitive topic that affects hundreds of thousands. Even if you aren't a surrendering birth parent, an adoptee, or directly impacted in some other way by a birthchild experience, unwanted separations touch us all—especially when people's rights are stripped away. When lies and deceit are involved, pain is magnified. This is why I became an adoption reform advocate.

Chosen

Adoption is not a guarantee of a better life, only a different life. Adoptive parents are not immune to divorce, alcoholism, financial disaster, job loss, etc. There is no guarantee that just because a child is adopted to a family with resources, that the boy or girl will have a superior life. It's truly a crap shoot.

For many adoptees, adoption feels like a life sentence, where their punishment is not knowing the truth about their origins. There is no one, singular universal adoption experience.

Many want to make a case for open adoption, however open adoption is not legally enforceable, and statistics show that most close in the first five years. Take a second and really think about this—what do you think is going through a child's mind in an open adoption?

I get to see my real Mommy, but go home to another Mommy?

Now, while the child is small, this may work for a while and give the adults what they want. But as the child grows older and begins to understand they have another family, but they can't live with them, how does it make them feel? Isn't adoption about the best interests of the child? Why do we throw harmful words around such as "chosen" for example?

In a child's mind, to be chosen means someone had to "un-choose" them first. Why aren't we spending more time listening to the voices of the adopted? Therapists' offices are filled with adoptees. Suicide rates are extremely high in adoptees as well.

Family Preservation

An average adoption costs anywhere between $40,000.00-$60,000.00. But what if we helped more mothers and children stay together versus so quickly taking infants away from their families? What if the church 'adopted' both parent and child, and helped the mother get on her feet, provided a stable home, and offered education and love beyond just the 'taking' of a child. What if society didn't work so hard to erase the original identity of a child and try to force it into something else?

Based on personal experience, and from hearing the hearts of many others, I believe family preservation should always be the first priority and adoption the last resort. The preferred method should be legal guardianship allowing the infant/child to be cared for by the adoptive family, while allowing their identity and first family to remain a part of their life. No falsified birth records should replace the truth, but perhaps an additional document could show the adoptive parents' names.

Adoptions should be ethical, void of any effort to coerce or persuade a young mother and/or father to relinquish their child due to lack of resources alone. If someone really wants to parent, they should look to foster children or true orphans, and not buy warm, wet infants, who are then erased in records, as if they were born to their adoptive parents.

Adoption will always exist, I understand that. There will always be a child in need, but it must be done honorably and without any kind of misrepresentation, persuasive tactics, or pressuring.

Due to the potential for subtle gas lighting or manipulation, adoptive parents should not be allowed in the delivery room. A mother may change her mind and feel guilty about disappointing the adoptive parents, otherwise.

If there is a waiting period after birth, allowing the mother to fully understand the seriousness of her decision, then and only then should the adoption process begin. After all, we don't take puppies from their mothers until they are at least six to eight weeks old—so why do we take an infant from its mother's breast immediately after birth. How does that make sense?

Adoption Truths

The closed adoption era caused horrific losses to millions of adoptees and their families. Some adoptees, not knowing their families' medical histories, chose not to have children. How sad is that? Male and female adoptees have lost their lives, because they didn't have basic health information about themselves that we, the non-adopted, take for granted.

What about passports?

Did you know that many adoptees are held captive in their own country because they cannot obtain their original birth certificates due to post 9/11 requirements? Social security and pensions are often affected by adoption as well. Many adoptees find out they were born in a different year, when they finally uncover the truth about their birth. Think about the problems that causes.

Another issue many wish to avoid is incest. I have heard countless stories of unknown family members dating and marrying their half siblings and cousins.

Birth certificates, for some, are an outright embarrassment. Did you know that many adoptee birth certificates were stamped illegitimate and bastard in years past?

Adoption is as layered as an onion.

Every one of us should be entitled to a clean and honest certificate of birth, not one that has been altered in any way. No human being should be denied that little piece of paper representing their origins, due to how they came into the world. Birthmother confidentiality is a myth many legislators hide behind to justify their continuance of a broken process. But with the power of social media and advanced DNA testing, adoptees are finding more ways to find and speak their truth. Thankfully, not all legislators support this archaic and pain-filled pattern.

Adoption Reform

One of the highlights of sharing my story, came from meeting with Vice President (then-Governor of Indiana), Mike Pence. We met in his office with the Speaker of the House and two board members from the agency I work with. Mr. Pence held both of my hands and intently listened to me as I explained why the records for our state had to open. It pleased me, many adoptees, and birth family members to have his support.

The official opening of Indiana birth records took place on July 1, 2018.

In 2020, the organization I co-founded along with Pam Kroskie, Indiana Adoptee Network, will hold its 4th annual conference. After previously speaking to adoptees, birthparents, and therapists from across the US and three other nations, I've served as an expert in birth family reunions, on an adoption panel, and presented workshops on the realities of reunions, offering both truth and hope, while challenging the current system. We must reform current adoption methods.

I've been touched by many people, seen families reunited, and made friendships with mothers, fathers and adoptees all across the US, Canada, Australia, England and Ireland. Most kept secrets like the ones in my shoebox, that prevented them from living peace-filled, healthy lives. Together, we stand in our sacred place, support each other in truth by the way of forgiveness, and give each other permission to finally release ourselves from years of emotional punishment.

Recently, my friend, co-author and adoptee, Pam Kroskie, and I released our children's book, *Frankie and Friends Talk Adoption.* We are currently developing other educational resources, including a coloring book for young adoptees, so they can express their feelings through play therapy. We also have other titles in the works, such as, *Frankie Gets a Brother*, *Frankie Talks to God About 'doption*, and *Frankie Meets His First Mom.*

SHOEBOX SHERPA

Using my signature brand, The Shoebox Sherpa, I guide those affected by adoption toward healing their past and empowering their future. Through coaching, training, and speaking at churches, book clubs, organizational conferences, workshops, and retreats, I get to help many people find their way out of the shoebox effect to true surrender. As I've shared, my expertise was conceived in experience.

I want you to know this—there's *magic in your mess*. You may have to sit in it for a bit or sift through all the broken pieces of your life, but those dysfunctional shards and your distorted sense of self, are actually the makings of a new, stronger, and better you. Whether your pain came from the heartache of a lost love, divorce, a financial mess, regret from poor choices, or anything else, we've all been through something. Life is messy, that's a fact, but that messiness offers you opportunities to regroup, acknowledge your Hiraeth, and stand in your sacred place.

Denial is a mask the wounded wear. For me, once I shed the role of the consummate actress and stepped into my truth—all of it—I was able to shed the emotional shackles that kept me a prisoner for decades. I finally found my clarity and purpose.

God doesn't promise us a Hallmark ending. But he does promise us he will never leave us during our darkest hours. Rethinking the shoebox effect saved my life. And it can save yours, too. If you are hurting and lost, grieving for the lost places of your past, know there is a way back to joy. Let me help you. Let me show you.

You know what you really want! Now lift that lid off and clean out *your* shoebox. The freedom you hunger for is hiding in plain sight—it's called the truth.

Your Shoebox Sherpa

ACKNOWLEDGMENTS

This book would not have been possible without the love, support and encouragement of many. Writing a book is not something you do overnight and is much harder than it looks. It took an entire team to bring my story to life.

My deepest appreciation goes out to my family—Jessica, Roger, Michele, Chelsea, Mackaila, Zane, Katie, and my cousin, Angie. Thank you for putting up with me for all these years. A special recognition to my mom who was there for me the last two years with coffee, tissues, and late-night talks. You got me through when I wanted to give up. I cannot thank you enough for all of your wise advice throughout the years. You are, and will ever be, my best friend. Thank you for always being my number one fan and never giving up on me. Mom, you are my rock. We did it!

Thank you to my longtime friends and colleagues for their continued support—Dana, Becky, Fran, Kathy, Domi, Jeremy, Stephanie, and Rhonda.

A big shout out to my other family, the adoption community. All of you are very special to me, and I am forever grateful for your love and support. Pam Kroskie, you have been with me since the very beginning in 2009. You've witnessed the struggles and encouraged me through difficult times.

Jennifer Fahlsing, Dr. Joyce Maguire Pavao, Patti Hawn, Anne Heffron, Sherrie Eldridge, Suzanne Bachner, Bob Brader, Rhonda Churchill, Lorraine Dusky, Rich Urlaub, Pamela Karanova, Linda

Franklin, David Bohl, Lynn Johansenn, Paige L. Adams Strickland, Adam Pertman and Lynn Grubb—to all of you, please know that your support, expertise, and friendship has not gone unnoticed.

To my fellow authors and coaches, thank you for your wisdom and experience—Vanessa Collins, Victoria Duerstock, Michelle Medlock Adams, Bethany Jett, Rhonda Robinson, Linda Joy Meyers, Dennis Lowery, Leslie Moise, Melissa L., and the #WritingCommunity.

To my amazing publishing team at Brookstone Creative Group. Thank you from the bottom of my heart for making my dream come true—Suzanne Kuhn, Anita Agers Brooks, Andrew Pino, Melinda Martin, Robin Hakanson Grunder, and the rest of the Brookstone team.

Finally, I couldn't leave out the one who inspired it all, the one who started me on my path to *The Shoebox Effect*—my beautiful golden retriever, Dreyfus. Because of you, my life has been transformed, I am forever grateful to have had you in my life. RIP, buddy.

CPSIA information can be obtained
at www.ICGtesting.com
Printed in the USA
LVHW012139310721
694024LV00012B/1176

9 781949 856170